Alfred's

Teach Yourself Pro Tools LE

AF869872

MICHAEL DEMUS

Everything you need to know to start recording now!

- For beginners with no prior training
- Covers the basics of MIDI setup, loops, microphones, recording guitars & vocals, effects, mixing, and more
- DVD includes over 110 minutes of video lessons

Alfred

Alfred Music Publishing Co., Inc.
P.O. Box 10003
Van Nuys, CA 91410-0003
alfred.com

Produced in association with Lawson Music Media, Inc.

ISBN-10: 0-7390-6640-4 Book & DVD
ISBN-13: 978-0-7390-6640-9 Book & DVD

Cover photos: Electric guitar courtesy of Fender Musical Instruments • Electronic keyboard courtesy of Korg USA, Inc.

Edited by Mary Cosola.

Alfred Cares. Contents printed on 100% recycled paper.

CONTENTS

INTRODUCTION

Pro Tools has become the standard-bearer digital audio workstation (DAW) used by most professional recording studios around the world. Whether you are working with Pro Tools LE, Pro Tools M-Powered or Pro Tools HD, the basics of this DAW application are the same across each version and level. Using Pro Tools correctly can result in some amazing-sounding recordings, no matter if they are recorded on your laptop with a basic audio interface, or recorded in a state-of-the-art recording facility.

Once you understand the basic foundation of the art and science of recording, it makes no difference if you are turning knobs on hardware or virtual knobs on software. Sound recording, while an art, is at its core, a science. It is indeed a scientific undertaking to capture sound in a way that is pleasant to the human ear.

When you begin to record with Pro Tools, you'll find yourself learning techniques for miking your instrument, setting the EQ of your recorded tracks, mixing them together for your final release and more. Pro Tool does an amazing job of offering a suite of tools that allow you to capture your art in an intuitive way from the first time you use the program.

Whether you are recording for your own pleasure, using Pro Tools to work on recording projects for others, recording and mixing audio for video soundtracks or even voiceover production of commercials, Pro Tools is the professional choice of engineers and musicians around the globe. This edition of *Teach Yourself Pro Tools* uses version 8, although the concepts will apply to older and newer versions as well.

This book and accompanying DVD will guide you from installation, to your first session setup, all the way through some complicated concepts made easy-to-understand with instructions, images and a bonus full-length video guiding you through Pro Tools all the way to mix-down. When you complete this book, you'll find yourself making professional-sounding recordings with the confidence of an experienced recording engineer.

CHAPTER 1

GETTING TO KNOW YOUR MAC

The first thing you're going to really want to understand is your Mac computer. They come in all shapes and size these days, with power ranging from entry-level ability to enough under the hood to create many dozens of tracks for simultaneous playback. Before we get too far, it is important to understand the Mac you own and what it is capable of doing.

This DVD deals mostly with the basic concepts of Pro Tools LE for Mac OS X. However, Pro Tools LE for Windows has also recently been released, and its system requirements are also listed. Be sure to read the requirements for each because there are big differences.

System Requirements for Pro Tools LE for MAC OSX

About Pro Tools LE Software

- A qualified Digidesign Pro Tools LE hardware interface is required to use Pro Tools LE software.
- The Pro Tools LE interface must be connected to your computer to use Pro Tools LE software.
- Pro Tools LE supports the use of any single supported Pro Tools LE audio interface. Simultaneous use of multiple Pro Tools LE devices is not supported.
- Audio interfaces by M-Audio or any manufacturer other than Digidesign will not work with Pro Tools LE software
- Pro Tools LE software allows a maximum of 18 audio inputs and outputs, depending on your audio interface I/O capability.
- Many M-Audio devices will work with Pro Tools M-Powered Software, which is identical to Pro Tools LE.

Mac OS X 10.6 (Snow Leopard)

Pro Tools software versions below 8.0.3 are not compatible with Snow Leopard. Pro Tools 8.0.3 is a free update for all Pro Tools 8 owners. Version 8.0.3 supports the following Mac OS X versions, on Intel-based Macs only:

- Mac OS X 10.6.1 – 10.6.4 (Snow Leopard)
- Mac OS X 10.5.5 – 10.5.8 (Leopard)

Please Note: Pro Tools 8.0.3 software (and higher) does not support some retired products, including:

- Mbox (original model)
- Macintosh PowerPC Computers

Mac OS X 10.5 (Leopard)

- Pro Tools LE 7.4.2 or Pro Tools LE 8 is required for Leopard.
- Pro Tools 7.4.2 requires Mac OS X 10.5.3 or 10.5.4, and is not compatible with earlier versions of Leopard (not tested with 10.5.5 or higher).
- Pro Tools 8.0 requires Mac OS X 10.5.5, 10.5.6, 10.5.7, or 10.5.8, and is not compatible with earlier versions of Leopard.

System Requirements for Pro Tools LE for Windows

Windows OS Requirements

For more information on official Pro Tools qualification with specific Windows versions, go to the Digidesign website and click on the compatibility link. There you will find a compatibility grid for every conceivable configuration.

FAT32 Drive Information

FAT32 Volumes Not Supported for Recording with Pro Tools 7.4 and Higher for Windows

- Pro Tools 7.3.x is the last version of Pro Tools that supports FAT32 for recording.
- Pro Tools 7.4 and higher for Windows XP and Windows Vista do not support FAT32 for recording, but will continue to support FAT32-formatted volumes for playback and transfer.

Windows Vista

- Officially Qualified with Pro Tools LE & M-Powered 7.4 & 8.0.x
  - Windows Vista Business or Ultimate Edition (32-bit OS Installation Only)
- Not Supported:
  - Windows Vista 64-bit (any version)
- Not Tested:
  - Windows Vista Home and Home Premium Edition
  - Although Windows Vista Home and Home Premium Edition have not been tested or qualified by Digidesign, there are currently no known issues with Vista Home and Home Premium 32-bit operating systems and Pro Tools LE 7.4/8.0 compared to the supported Windows Vista Business or Ultimate Edition operating systems.

Windows Vista SP1

Pro Tools 8.0 is officially qualified with Windows Vista with Service Pack 1. There are currently no known issues with Pro Tools 7.4 with Service Pack 1 for Windows Vista based on our initial limited testing and customer feedback. Although Pro Tools 7.4 will not be fully tested with Vista SP1, we do not recommend against 7.4 users updating to SP1, given the number of important overall system fixes in SP1. We do recommend that you backup your system and create a restore point before updating to SP1, should you encounter any problems after installing the update.

Not Compatible with Vista

- Pro Tools LE and M-Powered 7.3.1 and earlier
- Avid video peripherals are not supported with Pro Tools LE 7.4 on Windows Vista. Pro Tools LE 8.0 adds support for the Avid Mojo SDI® (Mojo not tested).
- Pro Tools HD® 7.4 software is not compatible with Windows Vista. Pro Tools HD 8.0 adds support for Windows Vista.
  - If you are purchasing a new Windows computer and need to use Pro Tools LE or M-Powered 7.3.1 or earlier, check to see if the manufacturer offers the option to configure with Windows XP Home or Windows XP Professional preinstalled.

Windows XP: Windows XP Service Pack 3

April 23, 2008 — Digidesign has officially qualified Windows XP Service Pack 3 with all products listed as qualified with Windows XP Service Pack 2, including systems with Avid video. There are currently no known compatibility differences between systems with XP SP2 or SP3. All compatibility information regarding Windows XP Service Pack 2 also applies to systems with Windows XP Service Pack 3.

Pro Tools 8.0 is officially qualified with Windows XP with Service Pack 3 (not tested with SP1 or SP2).

Windows XP SP2, Microsoft DEP and PACE InterLok Drivers Update

- All Pro Tools LE versions for Windows XP require Windows XP Service Pack 1 or higher.
- Pro Tools LE 6.9 and higher require Windows XP Service Pack 2 or 3 (SP1 not tested).
- All versions of Pro Tools earlier than 6.9 install PACE InterLok drivers that are not compatible with SP2 or SP3.

In order to use Windows XP SP2 or SP3 with earlier versions, you must update your PACE InterLok drivers after installing Pro Tools software.

- If you encounter unexplained blue screens, freezes or spontaneous reboots when launching Pro Tools with Windows XP Service Pack 2, please update your PACE InterLok drivers
- The current InterLok drivers solve the described problems without having to disable Microsoft's DEP (Data Execution Prevention) feature introduced with Windows XP Service Pack 2

At the time of this writing, Avid/Digidesign has not updated their website with compatibility specs for Windows 7. To get those specs when they are released, visit Avid Audio's website at www.avid.com.

Hard Drives

A quick word about recording audio to different types of hard drives: DAW's (Digital Audio Workstations) take analog signals and convert them into digital information. This information is then stored onto a separate hard drive from the hard drive where the application is installed. Recording data on the same drive where your applications are installed will create major problems. Data hard drives can be located in extra bays in your computer tower or can be connected through Firewire or USB connections. Check the specifications of your computer to find out the fastest drive you can use in your system. Many studios use external Firewire drives. These drives are connected through the 400 or 800 ports and run at 7200 rpm. USB drives are great for storage but are too slow for recording live audio. Depending on your audio settings (which will be covered in a later chapter), these converted audio files can become very large not only in size but in quantity. So be sure to not only get a fast drive but one that can handle several projects at a time.

Finding And Understanding System Information

On the DVD that comes with this book, the examples shown will be on a Mac system.

Why is it so important to know this information? Pro Tools LE requires a certain version of operating software to run properly and a certain level of RAM, hard-drive space, and processing power to record, to use virtual instruments, and to use features of the program, such as reverbs and other effects.

▲ Fig. 1: About This Mac displays important system information.

Mac System

To find out more about your Mac, click on the Apple in the top left corner of your screen, then choose "About this Mac." This will cause a window to pop up where you'll see the version of OS X your Mac is running, followed by the processor description and the amount of memory (also known as RAM). You'll want to know these three basic things when comparing your Mac's system to the system requirements of Pro Tools LE.

If you choose "More Info" on that pop-up window, you'll find a more detailed list of everything about your Mac, listed under Hardware, Network and Software. The Hardware section will tell you about the drives, memory, added PCI or other cards, USB devices, graphics cards, and more.

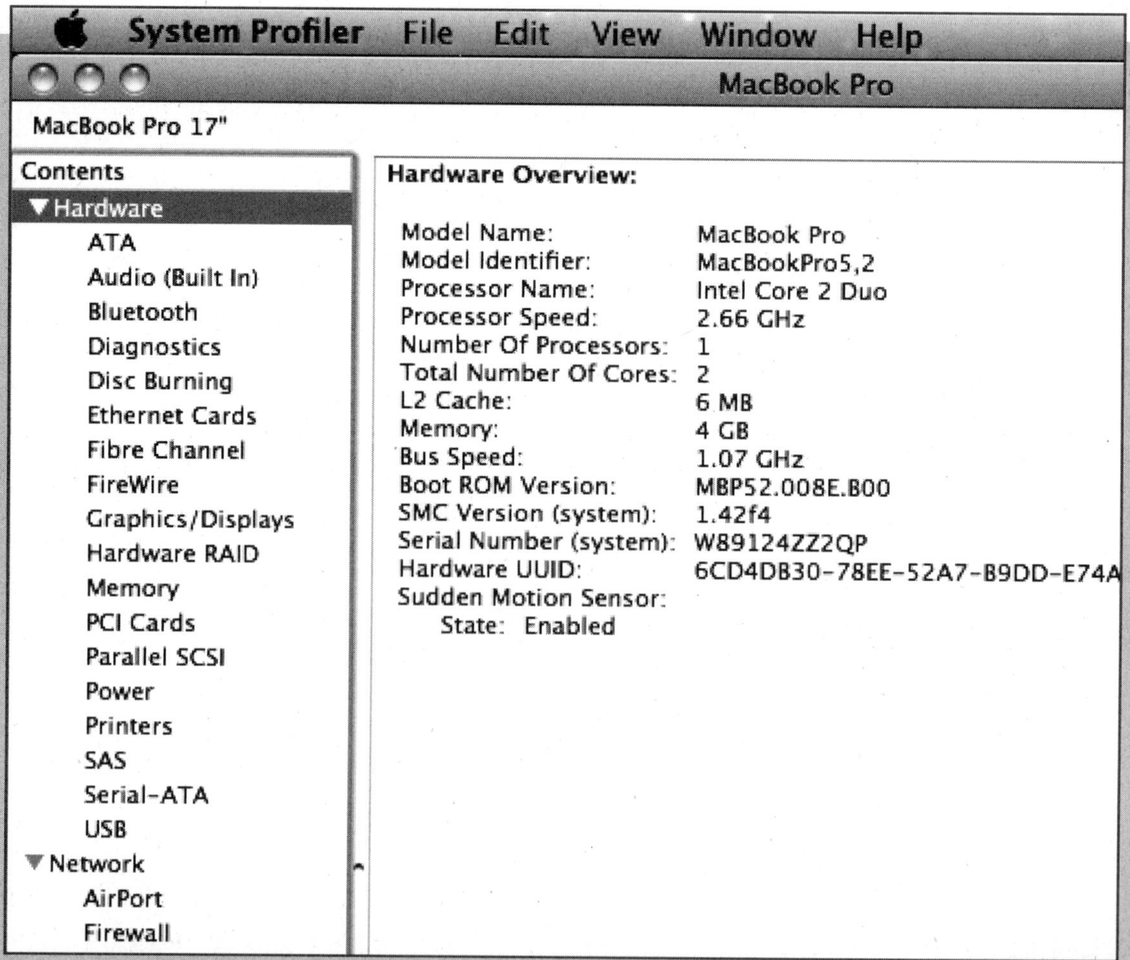

▲ Fig. 2: Clicking "More Info" on the About This Mac screen will show a detailed list of all your hardware.

If you've never spent time in your Mac's System Profiler, I highly recommend you spend a little time there getting familiar with your machine. It will save you many headaches such as buying a software package you can't run or can't run well, or trying to make a hardware device work with a machine that doesn't support it.

The amount of RAM you have and the speed of your processors (in addition to how many cores your processors have, e.g., Intel Core Duo, Core 2 Duo, and so on) directly relate to how many software instruments you can use and how many audio tracks you can create while recording.

In other words, don't expect to use an older Mac, such as a PowerPC G5 model, or even some older Intel-based Core Duo system, with not much RAM and expect to get 25-30 audio tracks and a bunch of virtual instruments. It won't happen. You can still get a lot done with Pro Tools LE running on most any Mac that meets the minimum requirements, but you'll be able to do even more if your Mac has the maximum amount of RAM it can hold and a faster, newer processor.

That's just how it is in the world of digital media creation. More power means more features and more tracks and toys available to create your masterpiece.

PC System

To find System Information for your Windows machine, click on the My Computer icon located on the desktop and then right click on Properties to see a listing of your specific configuration.

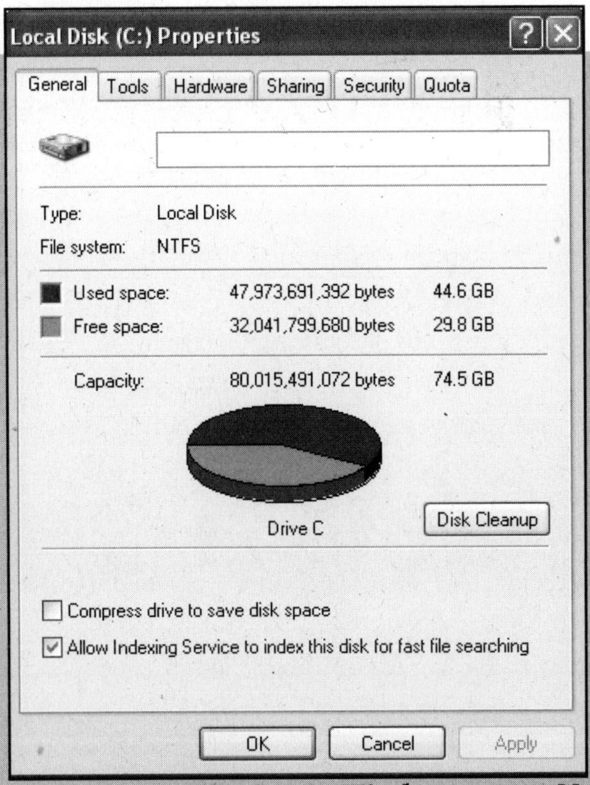

▲ *Fig. 2a: In Windows, go to My Computer, right click on the C drive and select Properties to get more information about your system.*

CHAPTER 2 MIDI AND PRO TOOLS LE

Now that we've examined what it takes to run Pro Tools LE and talked a little about your computer's processing power and memory requirements, we'll start to cover some of the ways that you can record sound with Pro Tools LE. We'll start by learning about something called MIDI.

MIDI, which stands for Musical Instrument Digital Interface, allows the input of data into a sequencing program that in turn triggers sounds assigned to that data and plays it back according to how the data was input. It can record notes, velocity, volume, and other aspects of the performance. In the past, MIDI was much more complicated, and sequencers were difficult-to-use hardware devices that talked to sound sources such as synthesizers and samplers via the MIDI connection. These days, MIDI is much easier to use, in no short part due to the development of USB connectivity, software-based synthesizers, samplers, and other virtual instruments controlled completely in your Computer.

Audio is different than MIDI, simply put, because a MIDI track has data in it that tells the track what to play from a sound source, whereas an audio track plays the actual audio recorded on the track. MIDI data can be manipulated in nearly infinite ways, whereas audio can be changed in much more limited ways using effects, signal processors, or other tricks. In other words, what you record with MIDI is not sound itself, but data to tell the computer what notes should be played for whatever sound you assign to the track. This means you can play a part as a piano, and go back and decide to make the exact same performance now sound like an organ or any other instrument, just by changing the sound rather than replaying the part with a new sound assigned.

With the exception of some new waveform-manipulation software just hitting the market, audio typically is a what-you-hear-is-what-you-get experience until you add effects like delay, reverb, compression, and so on to shape the actual recorded part into something different than how it was originally played. MIDI data, on the other hand, can be changed in an innumerable amount of ways very easily, and even a beginner can do it within Pro Tools LE.

A MIDI device gets data into Pro Tools LE tracks using a piano-style keyboard or, if you're brave, a MIDI guitar, MIDI wind controller, or other MIDI input device. These other musical instrument-style MIDI devices are much more difficult to use, but if you have the money to spend and are an expert at playing saxophone, clarinet, or guitar, you can always use a MIDI guitar or wind controller.

For the purposes of this book and accompanying DVD, we're going to assume you are using a simple MIDI keyboard connected to your computer or Pro Tools LE. (An alternative method of inputting MIDI using the QWERTY keyboard will be discussed later on in the book.) If you choose to use a different type of MIDI controller, the same principles will apply as with a piano keyboard.

If you want to record software instruments with Pro Tools LE, you can use pretty much any type of MIDI input device such as a MIDI guitar or wind controller, but the simplest is a MIDI keyboard. You can purchase a simple multi-octave keyboard with no built-in sounds, which sends only MIDI data via USB, for less than $100. This will more than suffice for getting your thoughts, ideas, and parts into your song.

If you don't use a USB MIDI keyboard or an audio device with MIDI built into it, you will have to buy a simple one-input USB MIDI device that connects to your computer, into which you will connect the output of your MIDI keyboard using a MIDI cable. This is done using a standard MIDI cable, of whatever length you need, which can be purchased just about any place that sells keyboards or electronics, from stores like Best Buy, Radio Shack, or your local music instrument retailer.

Many stand-alone digital pianos and keyboards still come with sounds built into them, some come with speakers built into them, and some even have sequencers and complicated recording systems as part of their system offering, but these features are easily replaced these days by software instruments, triggered by MIDI keyboards, running on a computer.

MIDI data in Pro Tools LE could be fed back out and into a keyboard with onboard sounds, causing the sounds to playback out of the audio outputs of the keyboard. These would be fed into an audio capturing device, just as you'd plug in a guitar or other instrument, for recording the sounds that come out of that stand-alone keyboard.

So if you have a digital piano with a MIDI output of some kind, using it to control sounds in Pro Tools LE will not get your sounds from that keyboard onto your Pro Tools LE MIDI track. The sounds built into your stand-alone digital keyboard or piano only come out of the audio outputs on the back of the keyboard that you would normally connect to an amplifier or P.A. system, so if you wanted to record them, you would be recording audio, not MIDI data.

Once you hear the sounds that come with Pro Tools LE, you won't want to bother with that kind of hassle. It's just not necessary, and it complicates an otherwise non-complicated process. Unless you just love a particular sound in your stand-alone digital keyboard/piano, I suggest sticking with using it as a controller for the sounds that come with Pro Tools LE.

Software Instruments in Pro Tools LE

So where will your sounds come from in Pro Tools LE? Well, Pro Tools LE calls MIDI tracks "instrument tracks." The program differentiates between recording a software instrument and live audio.

We'll get into track-level connection and setting of these devices later in the book; for now, just make sure you have a basic understanding of the hardware you'll want to own to get sound into your Computer and Pro Tools LE.

I encourage you to visit your local musical instrument retailer who specializes in recording or has a healthy pro audio recording department, versus a smaller mom-and-pop stores where recording is something they just don't know much about, because you'll likely be able to choose from a better selection and find a more knowledgeable staff to advise you on which device suits your needs best.

Arm yourself with an affordable Pro Tools Hardware option for Audio/MIDI capturing device and a MIDI input instrument you're comfortable playing, and you'll be on your way to making great tracks in no time!

CHAPTER 3 AUDIO DEVICES AND PRO TOOLS LE

Digidesign has devised their family of audio software to work only with their specific audio devices. There are so many variations with these devices that instead of trying to describe all of them in this book, it would be best for the reader to go to the Digidesign website and read all the information available. There seems to be a larger set of compatibility issues with all the different Windows systems and hardware configurations than with OSX systems, so that's why it is my strong opinion and suggestion that Windows owners go to the website and do a complete study of all the hardware compatibility and support articles.The majority of this chapter will focus on the MAC version of Pro Tools LE.

Audio devices take sound from an analog source and convert it to a digital source. Whether it's the sound of your voice through a microphone or the sound of your guitar plugged directly into an input, the sound starts out as analog, and the audio device's job is to convert it to a digital file so that it can be played back and manipulated by a computer, software, or a stand-alone digital recording device.

Audio devices take the audio signal you create with your instrument or microphone and convert that analog signal into a digital signal, which in simple terms means they take the sound you hear and put it into your computer.

It is really important that you verify that your Digidesign audio device works with your OS X version before you buy it. For instance, Pro Tools LE 8 doesn't work with anything lower than OS X Leopard 10.5.5, which means if the audio device doesn't work with 10.5.5 or Leopard, don't buy it.

Audio MIDI Setup in Mac OS X

The next thing you want to do is to get familiar with a feature of your Mac OS X Leopard system called Audio MIDI Setup. You'll find Audio MIDI Setup in the system hard drive in the Utilities folder.

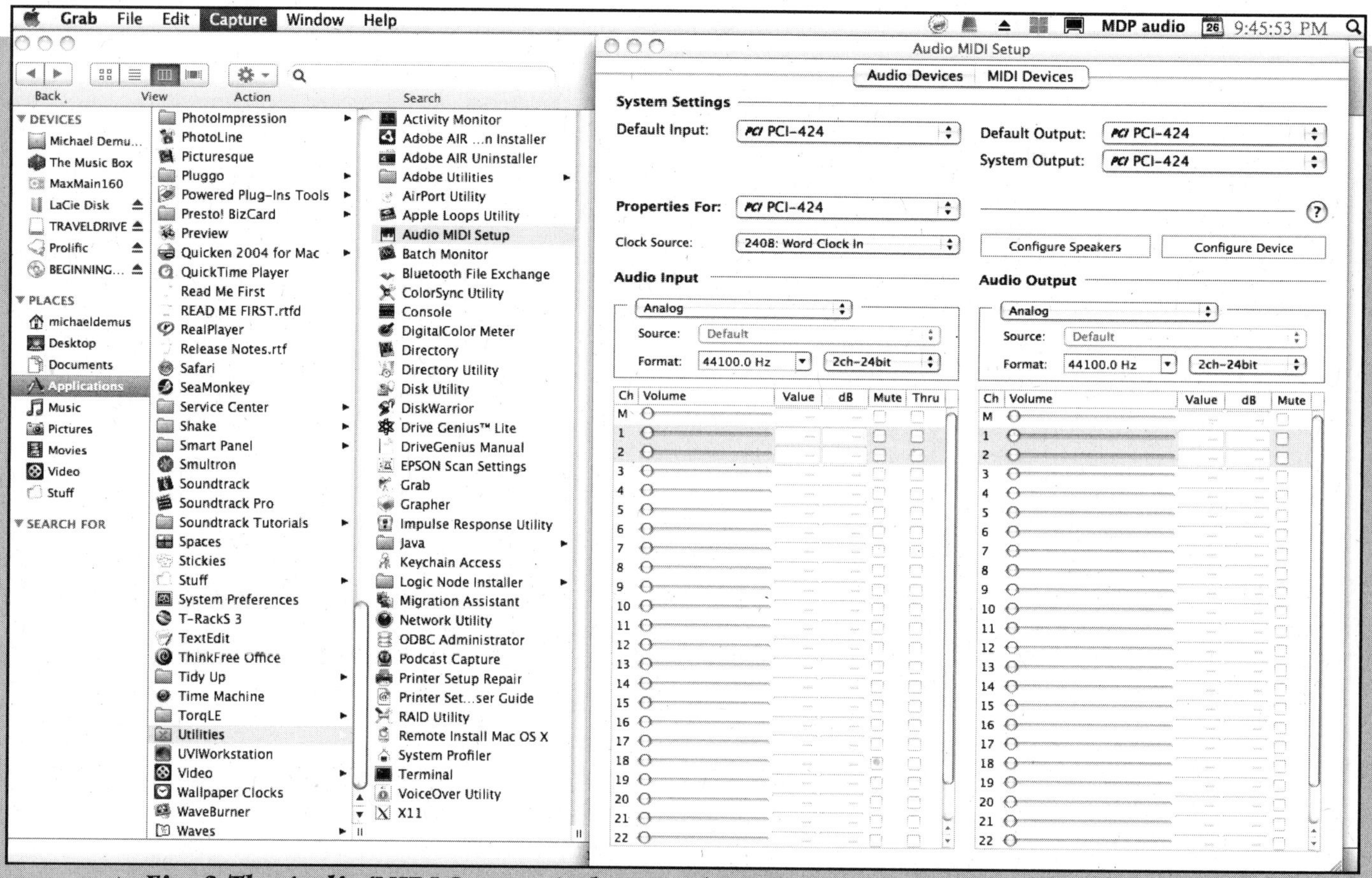

▲ ***Fig. 3 The Audio/MIDI Setup window is where you go to configure your hardware devices.***

Double-click Audio MIDI Setup to open it. With your audio and MIDI devices plugged into your Mac, your Audio MIDI Setup application utility should show them as present on the system.

Follow the manufacturer's instructions to install the drivers for your device if you are required to do so. This should be quick and painless. Following this, you should see the devices in the program, ready for you to configure.

If your device is not showing up, be sure you have installed its installation disc's drivers if required, check the power source if it has one, and check to see if the power button is pressed if it has one. If your device is listed, but appears grayed-out, you need to plug (or re-plug) the device into the computer. Once it's there and fully colored, it should be ready to use with your computer and Pro Tools.

If you're using a separate, stand-alone MIDI interface or the MIDI ports on your audio device, there will likely be some green lights that will flash when you hit a key on your MIDI keyboard. This lets you know that MIDI signal is being sent. You can also see the device light up in Audio MIDI Setup to show that you're sending data.

I Can't See My Audio Device!

If you don't see your audio device listed, it likely is due to one of the following reasons:

MINI LESSON

Likely Reasons You Can't See Your Audio Device

- It is not plugged in.
- It requires additional power to work and its not plugged into the wall or not turned on.
- It does not have the drivers installed for it from the manufacturer.
- It is a problem caused by the combination of the above items.

I know these steps all sound too simple, but check them first if you don't see your device. The same rules apply to your MIDI device. Sometimes you may need to restart your machine if it's acting wonky. And at other times, if your computer stops recognizing your audio or MIDI devices, it can help to unplug them and plug them back in. If that still doesn't work, and you know that the drivers are installed (if needed), everything has power, and it's connected right, you can do something called "zapping the P-RAM."

Often, if your Mac is behaving stubbornly, connection issues can be solved by doing something called "Zapping the PRAM" if you are using a Mac. If your device is installed correctly, the drivers are installed, the cables are connected, the power is turned on, and there is no logical reason your device should not be working, try re-starting your computer, and when you hear the first "bong" sound, simultaneously press the Option, Command, letter P and letter R keys and hold them down until you hear the Mac restart and "bong" again at least once or twice, then release the keys and let the Mac finish starting up completely before you proceed. This clears everything out of the parameter memory, which includes attached peripherals, and forces the Mac to recognize everything again.

Sometimes it may become necessary to "repair permissions" on your Mac. This is done in the Disk Utility application found in the Utilities directory, which is inside of the Applications folder. It's good to get in the habit of repairing your Mac's permissions when you install a new application. To do this, simply open your Mac's Disk Utility application found in the Utilities folder, select your hard drive, and then click Repair Permissions. If you are using a Windows machine, you'll likely need to restart your computer and reset your audio device connection by unplugging it and plugging it back in after rebooting.

Something else that can make a program or attached device go a bit wonky on a Mac is a drive with a file system that's become out of order because you've moved large files around, added and deleted lots of files, and so on. I can't stress enough the importance of owning a program called Disk Warrior, by Alsoft (www.alsoft.com). Disk Warrior can perform all kinds of tricks to keep your drive in proper working order. I typically will run Disk Warrior anytime I start seeing too many long spinning "pinwheels" indicating the drive is taking too long to access.

If you're going to be recording, you're going to be creating a lot of big files and moving them around, so you'll want a program like Disk Warrior. I bring this up at this point in the book because an out of order drive can cause all kinds of issues, including trouble recognizing devices. We had an experience at our studio where CDs we were burning using a program called Toast were burning only one channel of audio. When we ran Disk Warrior, we found the drive's file system was 37 percent out of order and let it repair the problem. Toast started burning CDs with audio in both channels again.

You should now have a rudimentary understanding of various Digidesign audio and MIDI devices, their types of connections, and how to make sure the Mac is seeing them. In our next chapter, we'll move on to choosing and using microphones with Pro Tools LE. If you're running Windows, be sure to keep your drive defragmented using your favorite disk utility.

CHAPTER 4

CHOOSING AND USING MICROPHONES

Let's talk a bit about basic microphone types, and what you should choose to get the best results for your songs in Pro Tools LE.

Microphones fall into three primary categories:

MINI PT LESSON

Three Types of Microphones

- **Condenser Microphones**. These are the kind of microphones commonly used in recording, broadcast media, and similar uses. Condenser mics typically require power from the mixer or device they connect to in order to work.
- **Dynamic Microphones**. These are the kind of microphones one would typically use in a hand-held situation or on a microphone stand for a live performance.
- **Ribbon Microphones**. A ribbon mic is a type of dynamic microphone. It uses a thin aluminum, duraluminum, or nanofilm ribbon placed between the poles of a magnet to generate voltages by electromagnetic induction.

Condenser Microphones

Condenser microphones work differently from dynamic microphones and are the preferred choice for serious audio recording. Condenser microphones are more sensitive and respond to a wider range of frequencies, allowing you to pick up more detail in your recordings and hear subtle nuances you might not otherwise capture with a dynamic microphone. With a condenser microphone, the sound enters into the diaphragm of the "capsule," which is made up of two plates. The two plates of the capacitor are made up of fixed and movable plates. One plate acts as a capacitor, and the vibrations from your voice or instrument produce changes in the distance between the capacitor's plates.

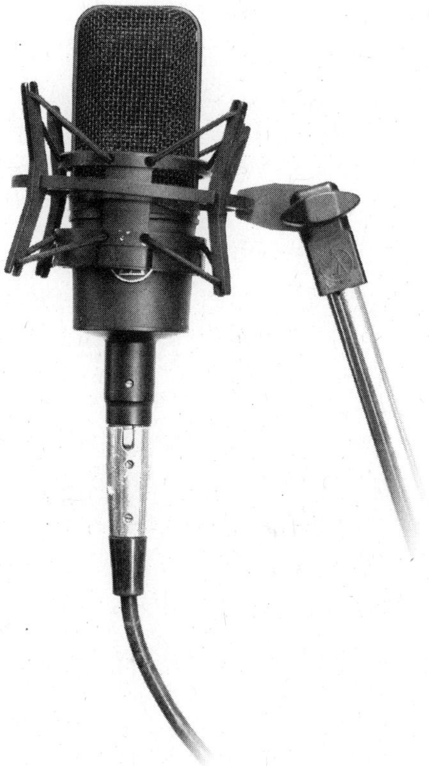

▲ ***Fig. 4 Condenser Microphone***

Condenser microphones can be unidirectional, meaning they are intended to pick up sound primarily from one side of the microphone, or bidirectional, meaning they pick up from both sides.

Some better condenser microphones, especially those that get their power from tubes, come with a power supply. These mics sometimes come with a rotating switch that lets you change the mic's pattern of pickup from a single unidirectional side to what's called a figure 8 pattern, which can create all kinds of interesting sounds for you to try. A figure 8 pattern grabs sounds from both sides of the capsule, which could open up the sound of your voice or pick up a guitar or other instrument in a whole new way that you may find appealing. Play around with the settings, and when you find one that sounds right, it is right!

Powering Up the Microphone

Condenser microphones require power to work. They get the power to put the sound through the XLR microphone cable from a number of sources. Most of the time, they get power from the 48 volt power button being engaged on your mixer or audio device. This is also known as phantom power.

Phantom power sends DC electrical current through a microphone cable to operate microphonesthat contain active electronic circuitry, such as condenser microphones. Phantom power is commonly built into mixers of all sizes, from the smallest to the largest, and is found in microphone preamplifiers and other audio equipment like digital recording interfaces for computers. Phantom power can also directly or indirectly supply the voltage used for polarizing the microphone's capsule. If its not engaged, the microphone won't make sound. It's the first thing to check when you're checking levels, and you should always have the sound to your headphones or speakers turned down, as well as the volume control for the microphone channel, before you push that phantom power button.

In some cases, the microphone might have a nine volt battery connection or an internal battery that recharges itself while connected to a power source. This isn't that common, but I do own some microphones that feature batteries, such as the Rode NT3, which can house a nine volt battery, or the CAD Equitek E-100, which has a rechargeable battery inside of it.

Battery-powered microphones are useful in rare situations where the mixer or recording device to which they are connected does not supply phantom power.

I've purposely left out a lot of the techno-babble that you probably don't care about right now. The goal is to give you a basic understanding of these kinds of microphones so you can make the right choice for what you plan to record with Pro Tools. I know you want to get the right mic to make good recordings with Pro Tools, so I'll cut to the chase. Buy a condenser microphone. You'll understand why as we move along and talk about dynamic microphones, especially the hand-held variety.

Dynamic Microphones

If you're serious about making great-sounding tracks from your acoustic instrument and voice, I am advising you to steer clear of dynamic microphones for most of the kind of recording you'll be doing at home. Will they work? Yes. Are they a good choice for recording instruments and vocals? No. There is no microphone I'd rather use when singing on a stage than a Shure SM58, the standard-bearer workhorse of live dynamic concert microphones. The SM58 is so tough you can drive a nail with one and it'll still work.

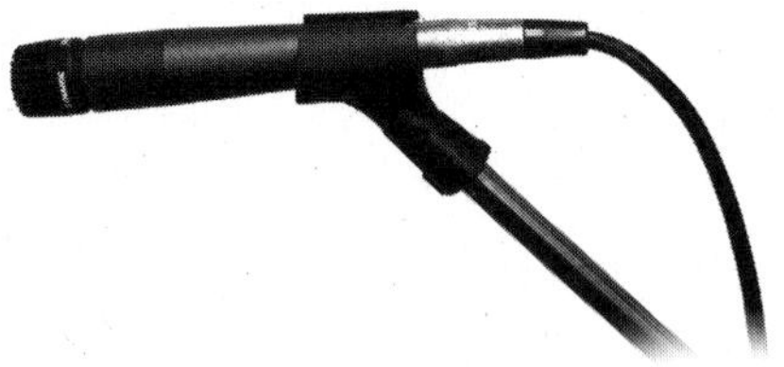

▲ ***Fig. 5 Dynamic Microphone***

Dynamic microphones are good for recording drum sets or recording guitar amps, but for instruments and vocals, they just can't pick up enough range to make your tracks sound their best. Why is that? It's all in how they work, which, as you'll see, is quite different from how a condenser mic works.

A dynamic, or moving-coil, microphone captures sound close to it by acting as a tiny loudspeaker wired in reverse. Instead of sound coming out, it captures the sound coming into it using a movable induction coil attached to the diaphragm, which is positioned in the magnetic field of a permanent magnet. If you unscrew the round windscreen cover from a Shure SM58 or SM57, you'll see what looks like a little speaker. And that's exactly what it is, a little speaker, only it's wired backward.

When you sing, the sound moves the diaphragm, which causes it to vibrate, and in turn, the coil in the magnetic field moves. This produces varying current in the moveable coil through electromagnetic induction. Dynamic microphones don't require any power to operate.

You can simply plug them into their cables and connect them to your mixer or audio device, then you're good to go.

Ribbon Microphones

Ribbon microphones are another kind of dynamic microphone, and some need power to work but most don't. Some hand-held models look like a dynamic microphone, and I used one for years in a live show setting, but it was a very controlled environment and it required 48v phantom power. My live mixer had phantom power, which allowed me to use it. You couldn't just plug that particular model in and go without providing a power source through your mixer, audio device, or microphone preamplifier. Most ribbon microphones don't require phantom power, but they do tend to need a lot of gain from a microphone pre-amplifier, also called a pre-amp or mic-pre. Check with the manual for your ribbon microphone model's power needs.

▲ ***Fig. 6 Ribbon Microphone***

Some warn you not to turn it on at all, others will require it. When in doubt, turn it off before blowing out your ribbon, especially in lower-end ribbon microphones. In many ways they work much like a dynamic moving-coil microphone, but they tend to be more expensive and sound their best, in my experience, with a nice tube microphone preamplifier. Ribbon mics are also somewhat fragile, so if you buy one, treat it very carefully. If you're interested in building up a nice mic collection, you'll want an affordable ribbon microphone in the mix, but that's not the sole mic I would suggest you own.

Why Choose the Condenser Microphone?

So why is a typical concert-style dynamic microphone not the best choice for recording when it works so wellfor live performances?It's really all about the range of frequencies that a dynamic microphone will capture versus a condenser microphone. A dynamic microphone simply will not respond linearly to the wide range of audio frequencies you'll want to capture when singing, playing a guitar, recording your favorite piano, or using other instruments.

You should take a look at and listen to both condenser and ribbon microphones, and always ask your local retailer to explain to you the value and features of each model.

A dynamic mic does not need 48 volt phantom power to operate, as a condenser mike will. It contains passive circuitry. This allows it to be used in a less-restricted manner, such as plugging directly into a computer's microphone input with the right adapter to give it the proper connection.

The best advice I have for you is to go and buy an affordable condenser microphone that sounds great for your voice, guitar, or other instrument. It will pick up the widest range of frequencies and produce a more natural, less colored sound that is closer to what the original source sounds like, allowing clearer, more accurate recordings.

Cost need not be an issue. You can get some exceptional recording microphones for home recording for under $100 these days, and for a few hundred dollars, you can get a professional-quality microphone that rivals the sound of those costing much more.

The trick is to find a pro audio retailer who is willing to let you put on some headphones and get into a space where you can sing into the mics without much (if any) outside interference, to find the perfect microphone before your purchase it. If they can't do that, make sure they have a liberal return policy so you can try the microphone out at home. A microphone choice can be a very personal decision, almost like finding the right pair of shoes to fit your feet.

In summary, I suggest that you get at least a two-channel Digidesign or compatible M-Audio audio interface that works with Leopard and has 48 volt phantom power, a pair of condenser microphones as good as your budget will allow, and a USB MIDI keyboard. Pair these with a good-quality set of headphones (don't skimp here; you get what you pay for), and some good playback monitor speakers. These basic tools coupled with a powerful Mac running Pro Tools LE can create some awesome recordings.

If you want to learn all about microphones and how to use them, I highly suggest a book entitled Professional Microphone Techniques by David Miles Huber and Philip Williams, published by ArtistPro Publishing.

With Professional Microphone Techniques, you can learn much more about the workings of various types of microphones and discover a wonderful assortment of ways to place mics on instruments. You can also listen to examples on the audio CD that comes with it.

CHAPTER 5 SETTING UP YOUR FIRST SESSION IN PRO TOOLS LE

It's now time to get Pro Tools LE open and ready to record something. In order to get to the fun stuff of making music, this chapter will not include how to install your software. Pro Tools LE comes with a huge amount of information that includes manuals, .pdf files, and online help pages that make the installation process easier to understand. So for now we will presume your software is loaded and ready to go!

As we mentioned before, Digidesign software will work only with Digidesign hardware. Some people think this is not fair because it is limiting, while others think it's great because it's easier to go from studio to studio if the hardware is similar. Most of the Digidesign audio devices are interchangeable; in other words, you can record a project on a full Pro Tools 8 HD setup and then take that session and open it up on Pro Tools LE and on one of their smallest audio devices like an mBox2 and, with a little tweaking, be able to work on it. On the DVD, David Terry is using an mBox2 mini, whereas I am using one of the original mBox devices, which believe it or not still works fine with my current version of Pro Tools LE. Your version may not be compatible with Pro Tools LE 8 or higher, so check with Digidesign's web site for compatibly. I would recommend getting a newer box however, because they are more powerful and efficient than the older models.

The mBox and the mBox2 mini are very similar, so unless noted these instructions will work for both boxes. Either device has two inputs and two outputs. On the back of the unit, you'll find jacks for line level input, instrument input, and microphone input. The front of the unit has a headphone jack for headphone output. We also have two gain controls for either mic or line, depending on what you are recording. There is also a mix knob that we will get into a little later. Let's check and see if the USB MIDI device has been connected correctly or not. We will also be able to see if the software is seeing the audio device you are using. Be sure and watch the DVD for tips on hooking up all your audio and MIDI cables.

Setting Up Audio and MIDI for Your Computer

Let's check out our MIDI and audio connections to the computer to make sure they are talking to each other. Go to your Applications folder and then open the Utilities folder. Scroll until you see the Audio MIDI Setup icon and double click on it. When the window opens up, you should see your audio device listed in the Properties menu. You can have more than one audio device in your system.

If you need to, choose your device from the list. Next, click on the MIDI tab and you should see your MIDI interface. If you don't see your devices, make sure you have the right drivers for both devices and that your cables are hooked up correctly. You should now be able to go to your keyboard and play a few notes and see your MIDI device responding to what you're playing. Again, MIDI devices have lights to indicate if MIDI information is be transmitted or received.

MIDI controllers are very popular and they are a great help in maneuvering around Pro Tools in a quick manner. If you have a MIDI controller, I am assuming you have a MIDI device that has at least two MIDI inputs and outputs. Move a fader on your controller to confirm that you are getting MIDI messages to your MIDI device. If you see some blinking lights, then everything is hooked up right, and we are ready for the next step.

As far as checking out the audio connections, if you can open a session, your computer is seeing the audio device. If you can't open a session, then you have a connection problem or a compatibility problem.

Setting Up Audio and MIDI For Pro Tools LE

Double click on your system drive to open up the Finder window. Go to your Applications folder, double click to open, and look for the Pro Tools LE icon. Double click on the Pro Tools LE icon. After the application has loaded, you will see the window shown below, which gives you some options to choose from.

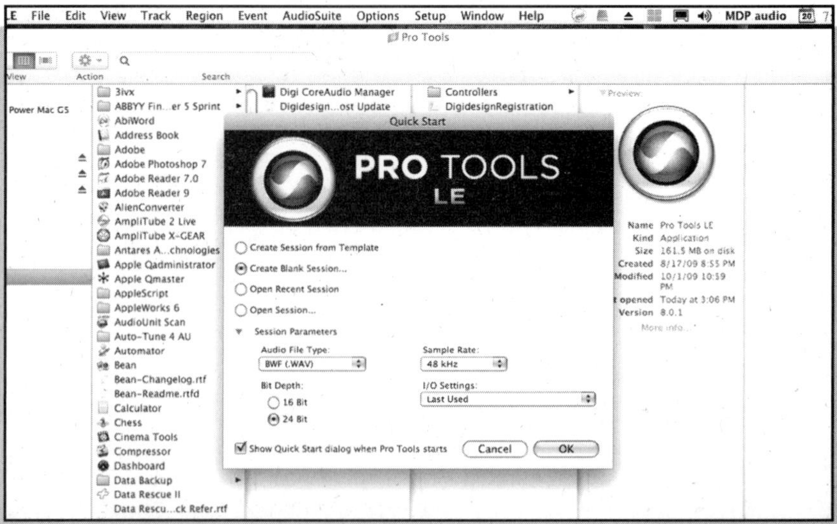

▲ ***Fig. 7: The Pro Tools LE setup window controls important global settings.***

This is called the Quick Start window, and you can check or uncheck the box that will tell Pro Tools what to do regarding this window every time you start up. There are templates of various kinds of sessions that you can use to start your session. You can open sessions already on your system or you can create a blank session. In order to create a blank session, you must select your audio file type, bit depth, sample rate, and input and output settings to get started. I must emphasize a few points about audio file type. In this writer's humble opinion, always set your session at the highest rate supported by your hardware. In this day and age, 24 bit at 48k is an excellent starting point because you get more fidelity and more headroom, which means you can push levels a little harder into your computer. Everything is running through the processor of your machine, so the higher the settings the better. Keep in mind that eventually your recording will be either mixed down to a CD, which is always 16 bit at 44.1k, or to an mp3, which is really low fidelity. It's my experience that if I capture my audio at as high a rate as I can, by the time it is down-sampled to CD or iTunes, it has a really good chance of still sounding like the original. It's also best to choose broadcast wav files. This is a cross-platform file format that works in either Mac or Windows and has a time stamp on it relative to the session in which it was originally recorded. If it accidentally gets moved, you can reinsert it into the session, and it will automatically go back to the original spot where it was recorded. That is a big lifesaver because, believe me, files do find a way of moving around every once in a while.

Set the bit rate at 24 and the sample rate at 48k. Leave the I/O setting at last used or stereo mix unless you have a multi input/output system connected to your software, and in that case select what you need from the menu. Click OK to first choose where to save your session. Find your external hard drive, create a name and then click Save. Now, Pro Tools will save all your files pertaining to this song in one folder. It will then create the main session file with the extension .ptf, and all the sub folders for your audio files, your backup files, and any plug in files that you use in this particular project.

▲ ***Fig. 8: Choose a folder where you want to save all files pertaining to this song.***

SAVE! SAVE! SAVE!

This is a good time to talk about saving your project. There is no perfect computer and no perfect piece of software. Trouble is always just a click away. Get into a habit of saving your project every few minutes. If you have to put a note on your monitor or another reminder somewhere easily seen, DO IT! There are countless horror stories of people getting absorbed in something they are doing and forgetting to save, and then all of a sudden you get the spinning beach ball of death. Fortunately Pro Tools LE has an automatic backup feature. Click on Pro Tools in the top window menu, choose Preferences and then choose Operation.

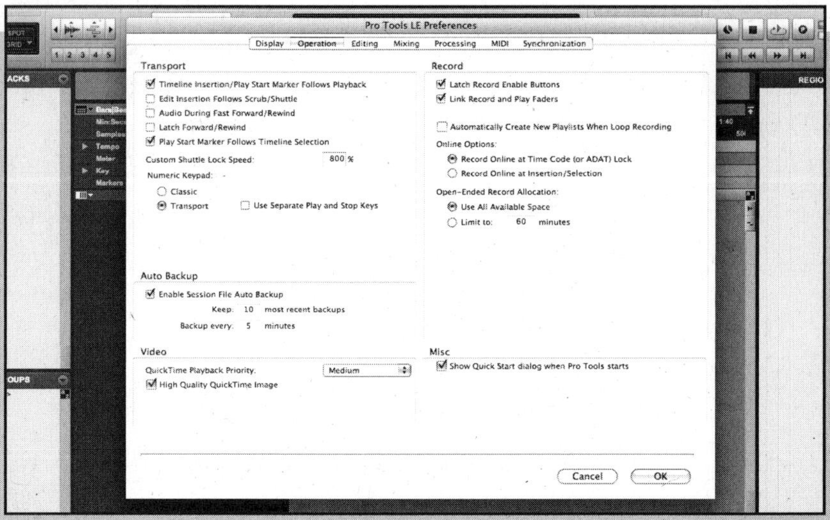

▲ ***Fig. 9: Do yourself a favor and check the Auto Backup option!***

Under Auto Backup, the Enable Session File Auto Backup option should already be checked. If not, do so now. Another good habit to get into is to be diligent in naming your files. Saving your files untitled can create a whole mess of confusion, because if you have several song files named Untitled 1, Untitled 2, and so forth, you will never be able to find anything.

Click OK to go back to the Edit Window.

There are only two main windows in Pro Tools LE: the Edit window and the Mix window. There are other sub windows for certain tasks, but these two windows are where you will spend the bulk of your time. One window we need to open before we proceed is the Playback Engine which you'll find under the Setup window in the main menu.

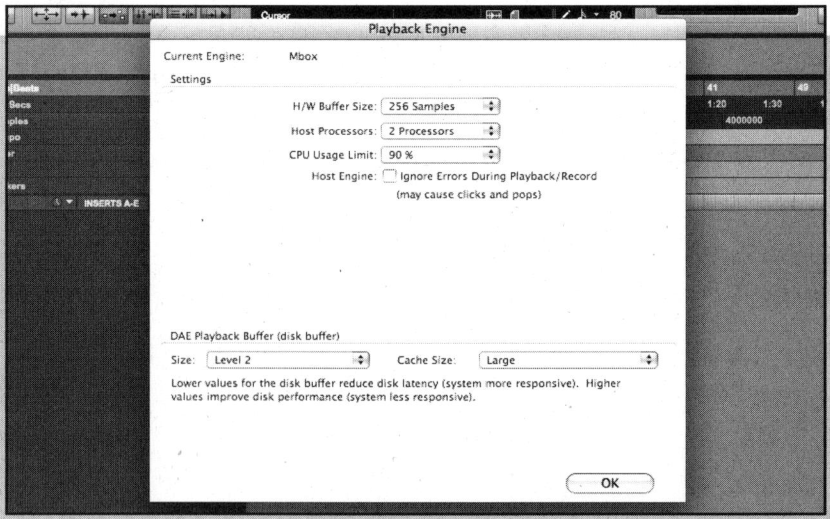

▲ ***Fig. 10: Finding the right settings for your system will take some experimenting.***

We need to setup our hardware buffer size. This setting is has to do with latency, which is a fancy word for delay. It takes a little time for audio or MIDI to travel through all the devices and back again to your speakers. Ideally, this setting should be low enough that you can't perceive the delay. Lower settings result in less latency, which is important when you are playing or singing along with an existing track, so you will need to experiment. Every audio configuration is different, and each set of variables will require different settings. There is no one-size-fits-all fix for all systems. When you're done recording and start to mix a project, however, you will want these latency settings at their highest so that you will have all the processing power available to you for the plug-ins you will be using. Read the .pdf files that came with the software about settings in the Playback Engine.

After making any changes, click OK to close the window.

Now that we have a working song title, have chosen where the files will be stored, and have our buffer settings where they need to be, let's get some audio and MIDI into Pro Tools LE.

Time To Record Some Tracks

Go up to the top menu, click on Track, and choose New. Click on the rectangular box where it says Audio Track and you will see several different options to choose from. For right now, we are only interested in audio and MIDI. Let's start by recording some MIDI, so choose Instrument track and Stereo.

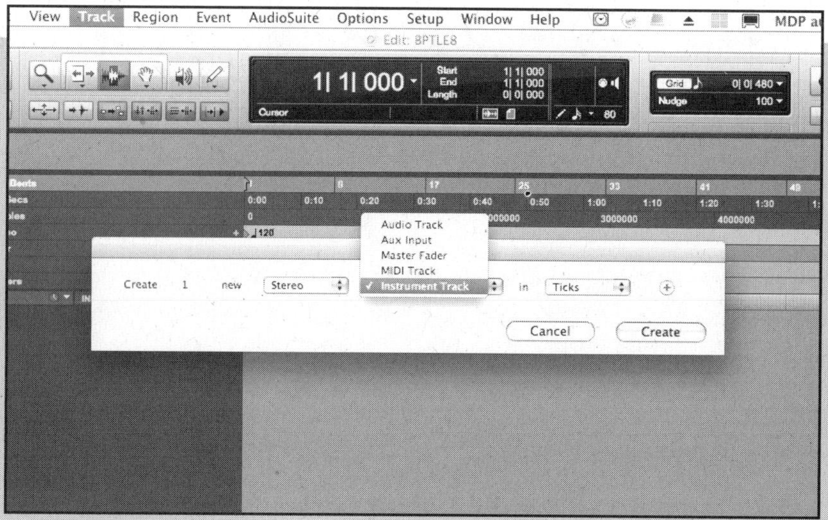

▲*Fig. 11: Choose Instrument Track.*

We are going to insert a piano plug-in, so we want a nice big stereo sound. Click Create, and the Edit window will now have an Instrument track.

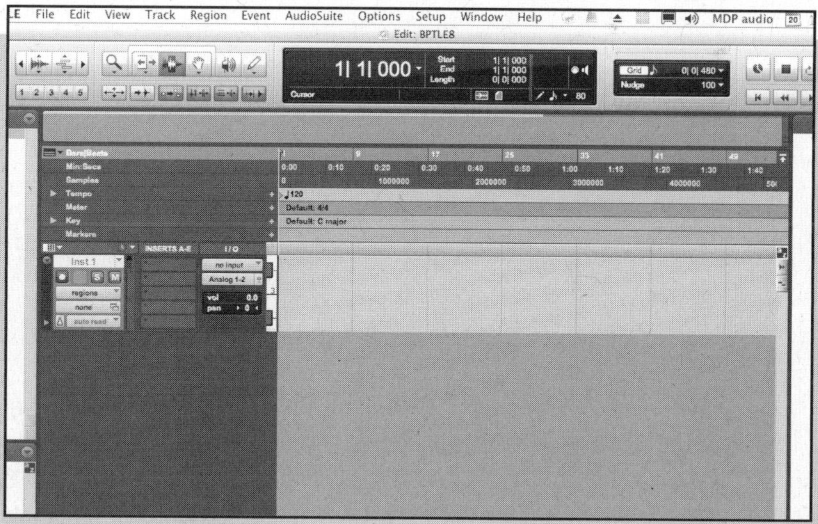

▲*Fig. 12: A new Instrument track appears.*

Place your cursor in the first box underneath the word Insert and click. Choose Multi-Channel Plug-In, Instrument, and then click on Mini Grand.

The plug-in window will open, then load the samples. Play a few notes on the keyboard once the little red line on the bottom of the keyboard window is gone. Play for a while and see how the software responds. You may or may not need to adjust your buffer size. When you are happy with the settings, close the piano.

▲ *Fig. 13: You can insert all kinds of instrument plug-ins or effects.*

Before we arm the track for recording, we need to name the track. You can find many horror stories of engineers forgetting to name their files and then coming back to a session and not having a clue where anything is. The same reason for naming song files applies to track names. Always name your tracks so you don't have 10 files saying Audio 1, Audio 2, and so forth. Descriptive names eliminate a massive amount of confusion and wasted time trying to figure out what your tracks are. Double click in the box that says Inst 1.

A box will come up where you can name the track, make some comments that will show up in your Mix window, and go forward or backward in your track list to name or rename other tracks. Type Piano or whatever name you choose and then click OK.

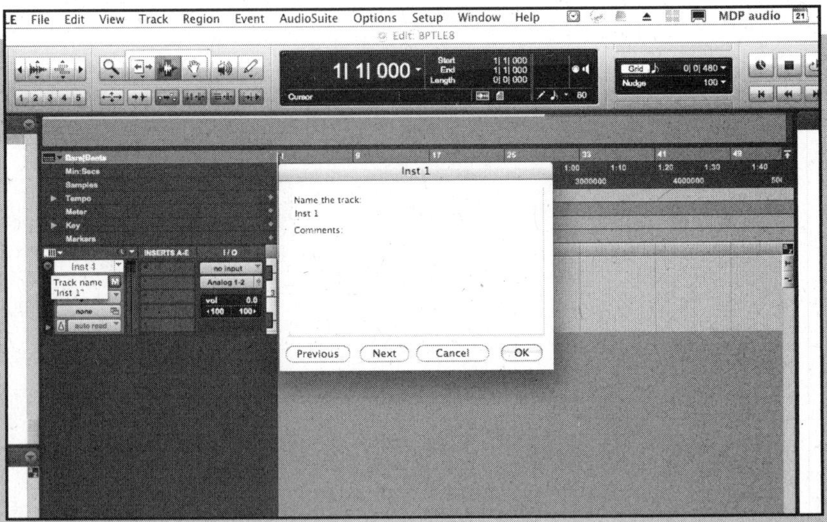

▲ *Fig. 14: Naming tracks will save a lot of time and prevent confusion later.*

Now let's check our audio and see if we're getting signal into our software and out back to our monitors. Click on Track in the main menu, click New, and then choose Mono, choose Audio, and then click Create.

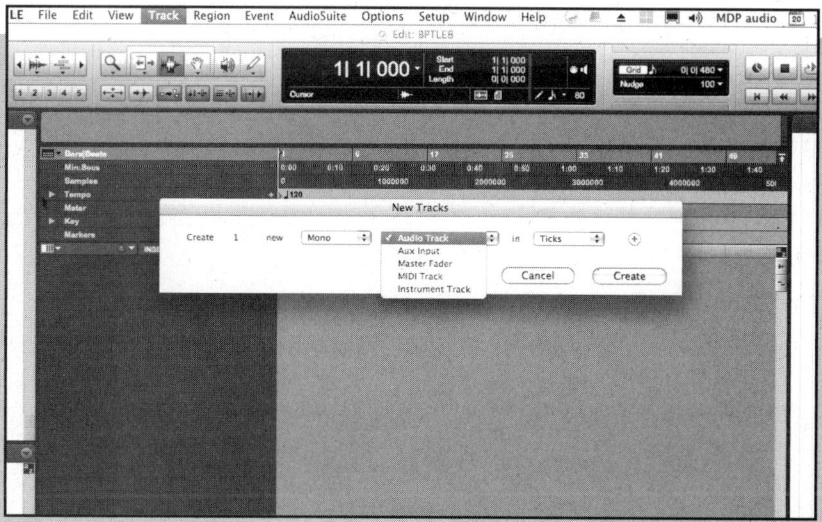

▲ ***Fig. 15: Choose Mono, Audio.***

Make sure you have Input 1 selected for input and Outputs 1-2 selected for the output.

The figures on the right show the basic audio setup for this demonstration. Arm your track by clicking on the record enable button (R) and then check your microphone by saying something into it. You should see the digital meter move and hear your voice through your monitors. If you see something but don't hear anything, check your connections from your computer through your audio device to your speakers.

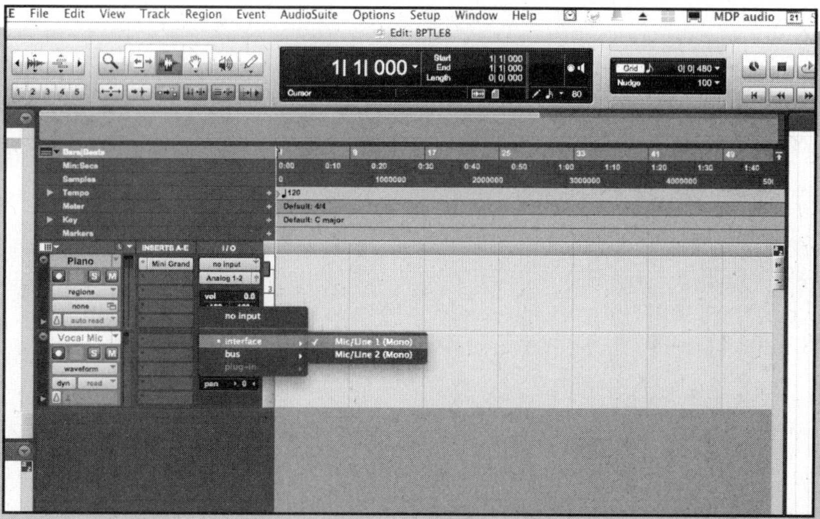

▲ ***Fig. 16: Select the correct input.***

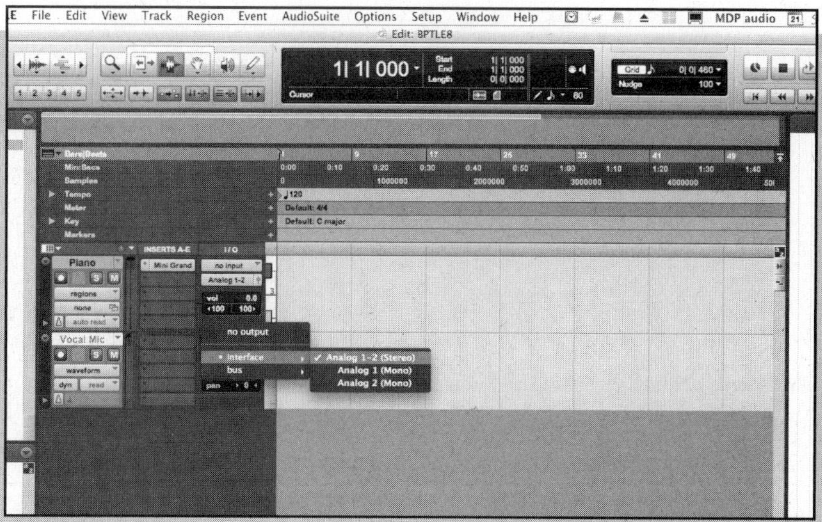

▲ ***Fig. 17: Select the correct output.***

Click on the main recording button and record some test audio. After you click on Stop, you should see a waveform and be able to play back what you recorded.

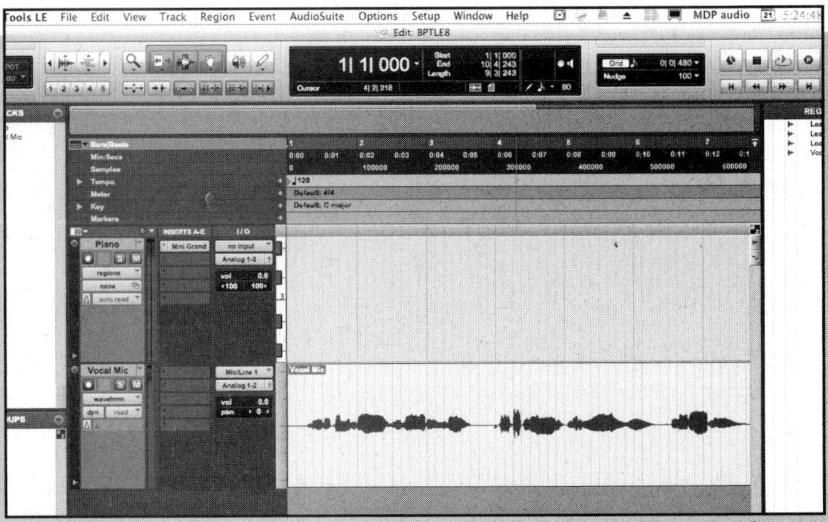

▲ ***Fig. 18: See the waveform of your recorded vocal test.***

If you have a MIDI controller, let's make sure it's installed. We are going to set Pro Tools LE to recognize a Mackie controller so we can use it to control the faders, pans, mutes, and anything else that can be controlled through MIDI. Click on Setup in the main menu, choose Peripherals, MIDI Controllers, and then click on the first slot to see a list of controllers. Choose your controller, the ports you are sending and receiving, and the MIDI channel. As soon as you close the window, your controller will be in operation.

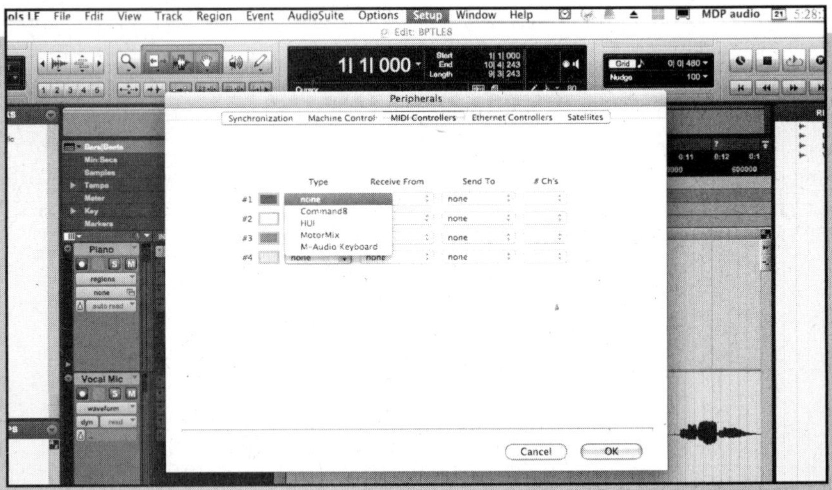

▲ ***Fig. 19: There is a collection of Control Surface devices available for use with Pro Tools LE.***

Now that we have all the basic technical setup done, let's look at how we can make some music in Pro Tools LE.

CHAPTER 6 MAKING MUSIC!

Now it's time to use some of the creative features of Pro Tools LE. Over the next few chapters, we will create a song where we will record audio and MIDI, and use the Pro Tools loop browser. Let's get started.

Let's create a new project like before and add an audio track. Save your track and give it a descriptive name. We're going to start by importing an audio loop. Pro Tools can set its tempo map based on the tempo information of the audio loop, so when you import it, the tempo will reset to the loop tempo and you can begin adding and overdubbing whatever you want.

First, create a click track. This is a very handy function in Pro Tools LE. Click on Track in the main menu and then choose Create Click Track.

▲ *Fig. 20: Create a click track.*

The Edit window will now have a track called Click. To make the track wider to see it a little better, use the + and — buttons in the corner of the window.

▲ *Fig. 21: Corner zoom buttons*

You can also click on the bar at the start of the track and choose a size from the menu list. If you hold down Option and click on this bar, the selection will affect all tracks.

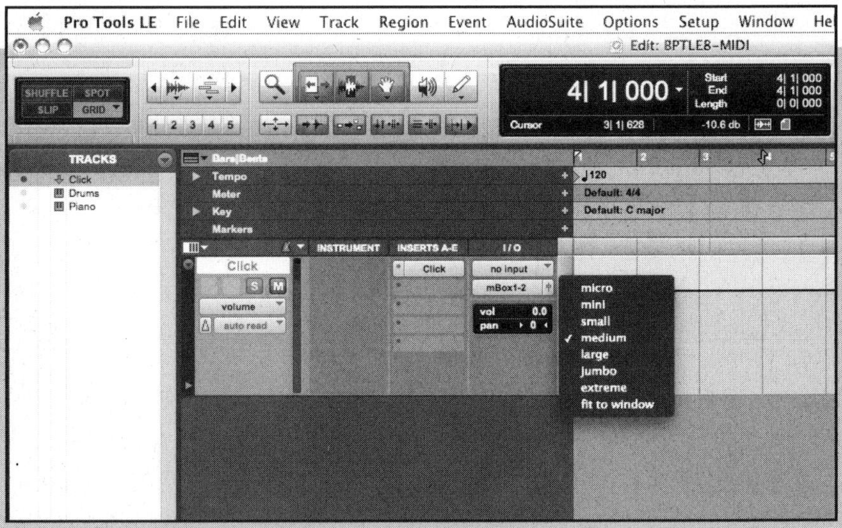

▲ ***Fig. 22: Track zoom bar***

Let's look around a little more. Click on the triangle just to the top left of where it says Click. This is where you can select all kinds of different options to display for that track. Click to put a check on whatever you want to see. Click on an option again to uncheck it and take it out of the channel strip. Since all plug-ins (including instruments) are inserts, click on Inserts A-E. The Click plug-in will be in the A slot.

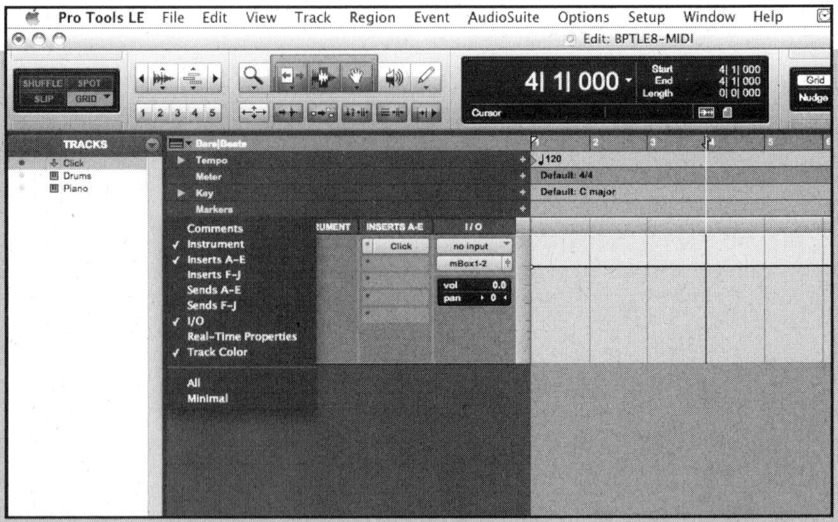

▲ ***Fig. 23: This is the Edit View Selector. Choose what you want displayed on the track.***

Click on the insert and the Click plug-in will open. You can tweak the Click however you want. Close the plug-in. If you click on the little dot to the left of the insert, you'll open up a plug-in folder and you can replace the click plug-in with another.

▲ *Fig. 24: From here you can select any plug-ins you have in your system.*

The same goes for all the other inserts. Just click on them and you will be given a menu to pick whatever plug-in you need.

Now let's import a loop in which we don't know the tempo. Our session right now shows a tempo of 120. You can click on Event in the main menu and choose Tempo Operations Window, which will open up a window for you to access several tempo options. I have prepared a couple of loops that I don't know the tempo to and put them on the desktop. When you click on File in the main menu and choose Import, then Audio, Pro Tools will ask you a couple of questions. First of all, you need to direct the Finder to the location of the audio is that you want to import. Since I put my loops on the desktop, I click on Desktop and click on the loop. You can see that there is some information displayed about the loop. Some files will have to be converted into single mono files to work in Pro Tools.

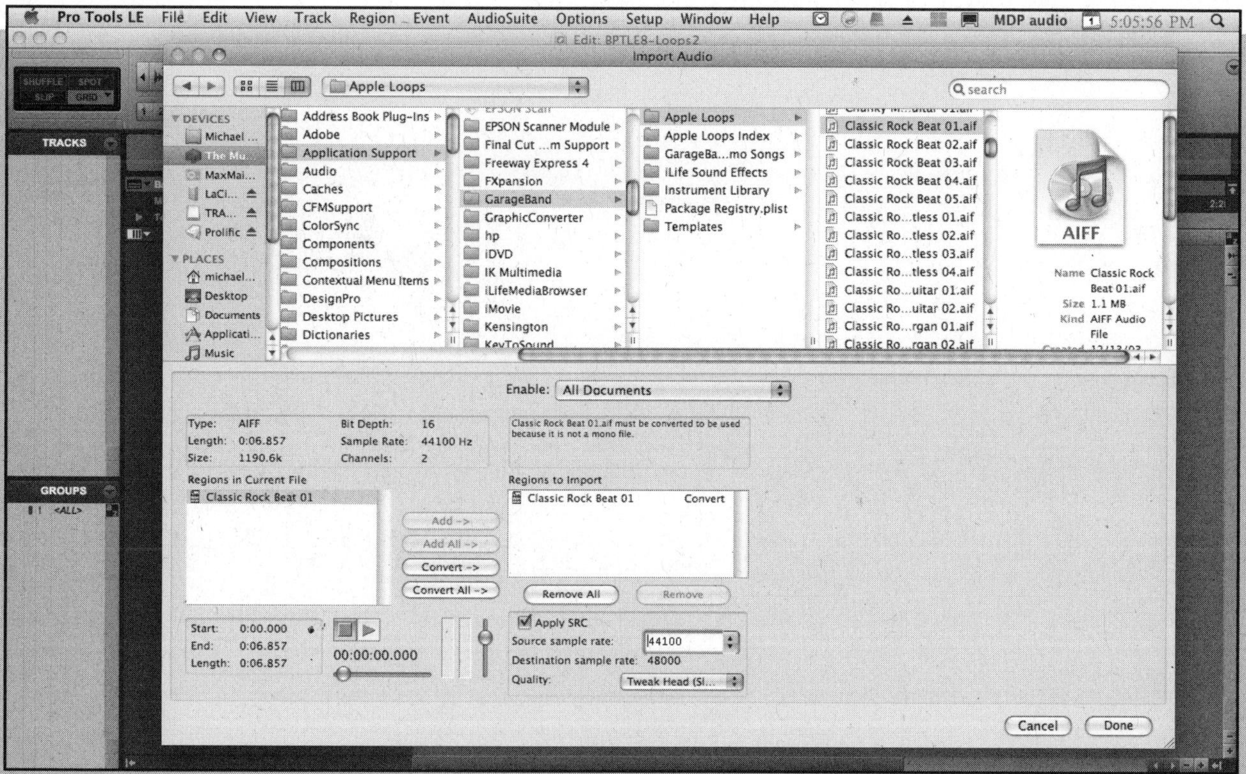

▲ *Fig. 25: Converting a loop for Pro Tools*

Importing Audio

Depending on the properties of the audio files you are importing, you can add, copy, or convert the files: When files are added to a Pro Tools session, they remain at their current hard drive location and are not moved or copied. The session references the original files wherever they are on your system. When files are copied into the session, the original files remain wherever they are on your system and are also copied to the session's Audio Files folder and added to the session. The session references the copied files, not the original files. When files are converted into the session, the original files remain wherever they are on your system and are copied to the session's Audio Files folder, where they are converted to the session's audio file format, sample rate, and bit depth.

The session references the converted files, not the original files. Mono and split stereo (or split multichannel) audio files that are of the same audio file format, sample rate, and bit depth of the session can be added to the session without conversion and with or without copying the files to the session's Audio Files folder. Pro Tools automatically converts files that don't match the session's audio file type, sample rate, or bit depth. Audio files that don't match the session audio file type, sample rate, and bit depth must be converted on import. Pro Tools also splits interleaved (when files are arranged to improve efficiency) audio files into multiple mono files. Once you have chosen which option you want, click Done. If you are copying the file, you will automatically be directed to the session Audio Files folder.

Tempo From the Loop

When you click on Choose, a window will come up asking for the destination of this file. You can choose a new track or region list as well as the location where you want to place the start of the file in the session. Leave it at Session Start. Regions are all the pieces of audio that you record or import and are displayed on the right side of the Edit window. For this example, let's leave it on New Track and click OK.

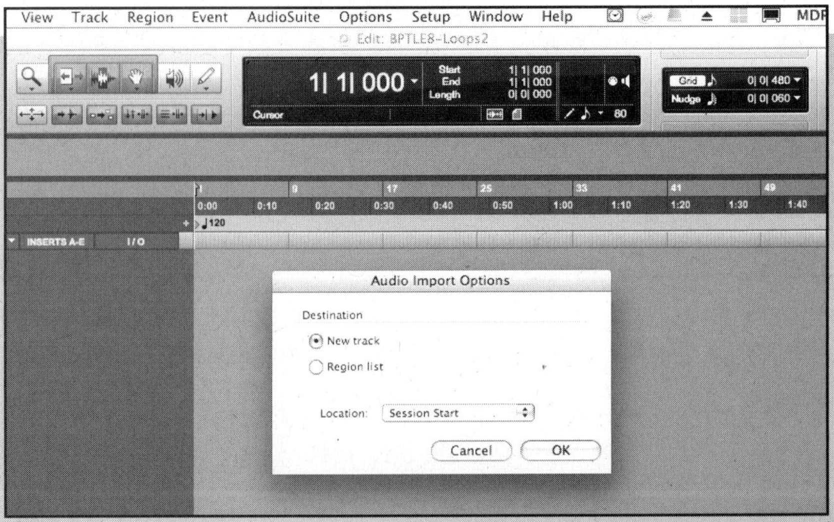

▲ *Fig. 26: Import New Track*

Now you have your loop in the Edit page, and you can see the waveform. At the top of the window is the Bars/Beat display. Just to the left, there is a rectangular box with a triangle. Clicking on the triangle opens a menu for you to choose what you want visible at the top of your window. In this example the Bars/Beat, Mins:Sec, Tempo, Meter, and Markers displays have been chosen.

To loop playback of your files, right click and hold on the Play icon at the top right of the window, and select Loop. This loop function will only work if you have one or more regions selected. We will talk about other ways to loop a little bit later.

Press the spacebar to play the loop, and you will hear that the click track and the loop are not in sync with each other. The loop is a four-bar loop and at the right tempo should fill all four measures. If we love this loop and want to build our song on it, we need to match the Pro Tools tempo with the loop. This is easily done by clicking on Event in the main menu and then choosing Identify Beat.

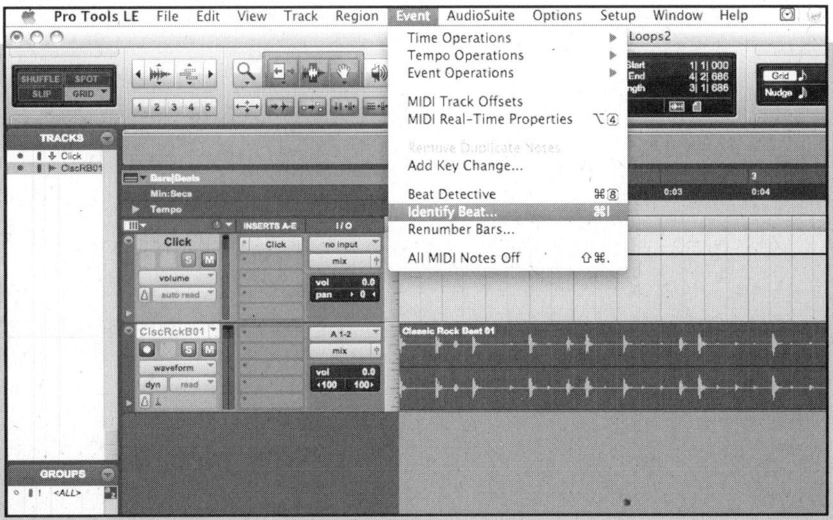

▲ Fig. 27: It's easy to change the tempo of a song to the tempo of an imported loop.

At this point, we are going to tell Pro Tools to adjust the tempo of the song to the tempo of the loop. Since the loop is supposed to be a four-bar phrase, change the End Location numbers to 5| 1| 000, which means beat one of the 5th measure. You can do this either by clicking on the number and typing a new number or by clicking and then moving your mouse to change the numbers. When you have changed the number, click OK.

Now you can see in the example that the tempo and the bar display have changed to match the loop. Instead of the tempo being 120, it is now 140, and the loop is four bars long. Play the loop and you will hear that is in sync with the click track. Now we can record audio or MIDI files, or import more loops to build on our song.

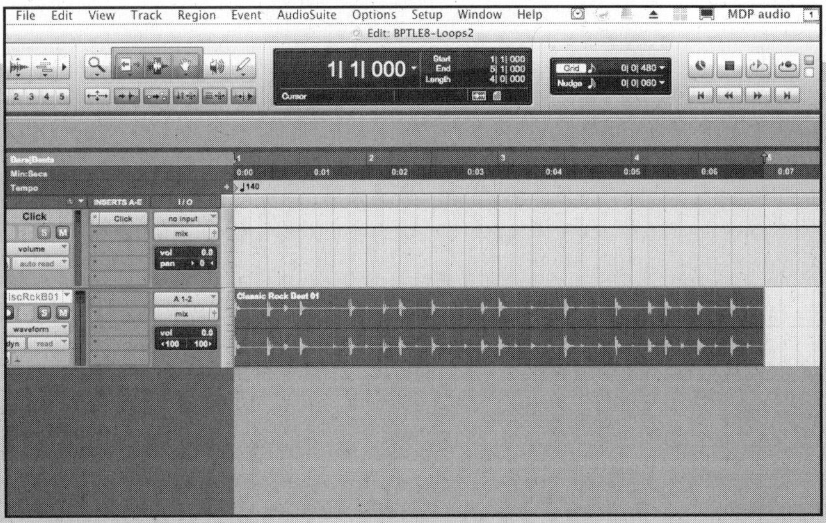

▲ Fig. 28: The loop is in sync with the changed tempo.

Following the Moving Tempo

Now let's go in reverse and make the loop follow the tempo. Sound impossible? Not anymore. Pro Tools incorporates Elastic Audio, which will take any audio and make it fit to the song tempo. Now there are some limitations. If you have a wide tempo range, you will hear audio artifacts or digital garbage. But if the tempo change is not too drastic, Elastic Audio is a great tool for finding the right feel in your song.

Just like in most software applications, you can use the Undo function to revert to the original settings, where the loop was inserted at the beginning and the tempo was at 120. Just underneath the box that says dyn, you will see a blue icon with a clock face. This is the time base selector for our track. There are two time base selections.

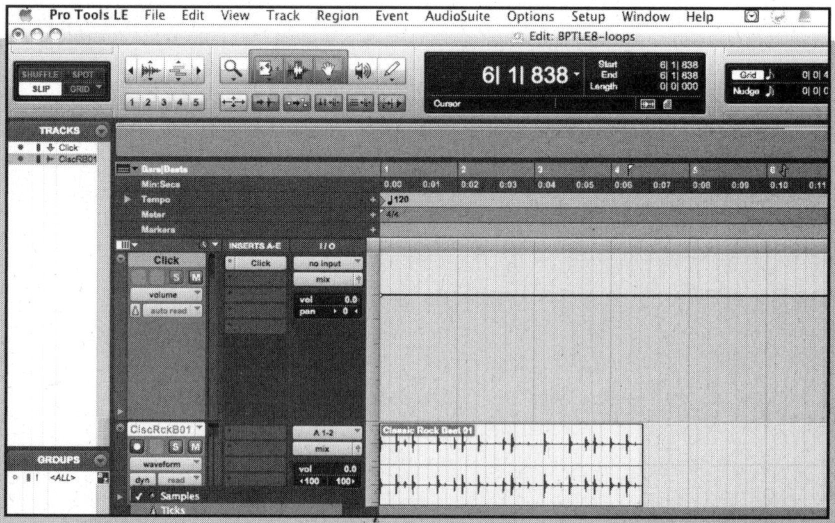

▲ *Fig. 29: Tick and Sample*

Audio tracks in Pro Tools are sample-based by default. This means that audio regions and events are located at specific sample locations and they do not move from that location if the tempo changes in the session–even though their bar and beat locations do change. MIDI and Instrument tracks in Pro Tools are tick-based by default. This means that MIDI regions and events are located at a specific bar and beat locations, and they do not move from that location if the tempo changes in the session–even though their sample location does change. You can go into the Preferences menu and make tick-based the default option when you import or record audio.

Click on the blue icon and choose the green metronome icon which is for tick-based audio. Click on that and you will see there are four types of Elastic Audio plug-ins. The Rhythmic plug-in is best suited for loops and drums. Choose Rhythmic and then when you see it in the slot, click on it to open its window.

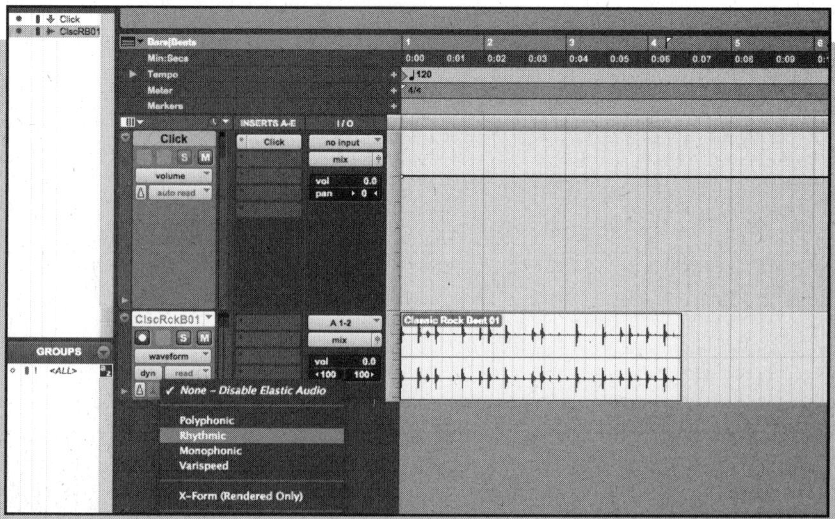

▲ *Fig. 30: Each Elastic Audio plug-in has a unique function.*

Now select the region and right click on it. A menu will pop up where you choose Conform to Tempo.

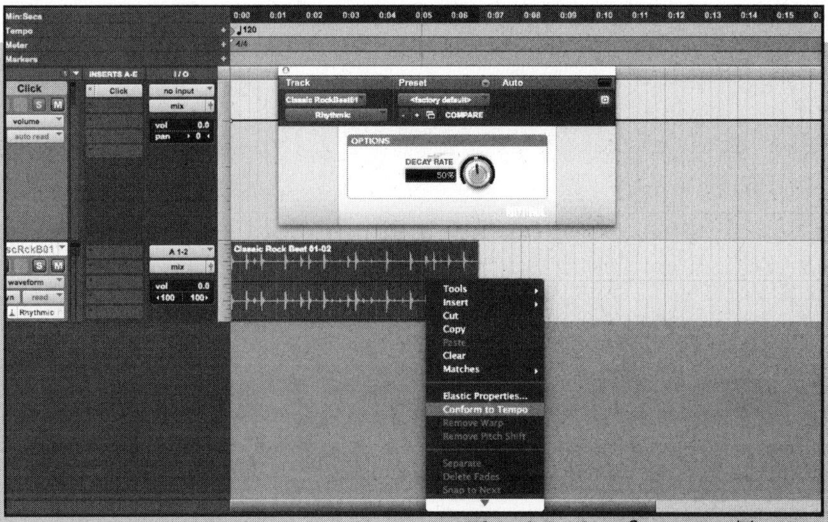

▲ *Fig. 31: Conform to Tempo*

When you do this, the loop will automatically adjust to the song tempo. In this case, it becomes a two-bar phrase instead of a four-bar phrase. Hit play and listen to your loop. If the loop for whatever reason is not sounding quite right, you can right click again on the region and select Elastic Properties. Here you can see the name and source information of the loop. You can also change the pitch, which can be very handy.

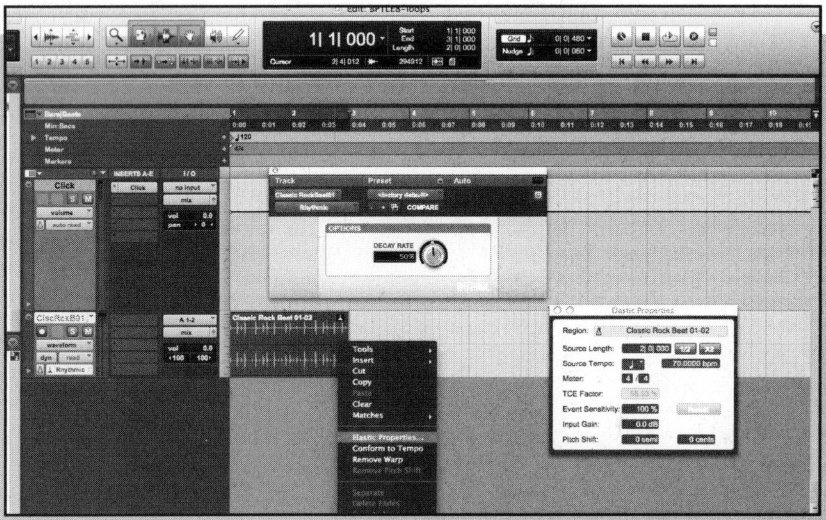

▲ *Fig. 32: More Elastic options*

Let's add a bass guitar loop. Again, for this example I pre-loaded some audio on my desktop; however, you can use whatever loops you have on your computer or on an external hard drive. Find your loop through the Import command, convert and copy it to your session folder, and then choose New Track for your destination.

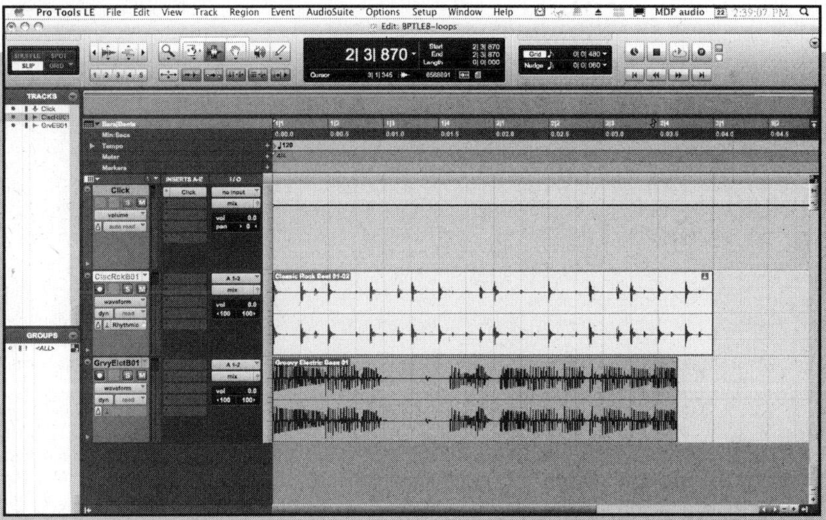

▲ *Fig. 33: Add a bass loop.*

You can see the new bass track and notice that it does not match the drum loop. Highlight the bass region and play the track. You will hear that it is not in sync with the drums. There is a little symbol in the top right hand of the drum loop region telling you this region is an Elastic Audio region. Go to the bass track time based icon and select Tick, then click on the insert and choose Monophonic this time instead of Rhythmic. Because our bass track is a mono file with pitch properties that need to be preserved, Monophonic is a better Elastic audio plug-in choice. Right click, choose Conform to Tempo, and watch the bass guitar region expand to match the drum region. Highlight a region and hit the spacebar to loop your playback.

▲ ***Fig. 34: Make the bass loop conform to tempo.***

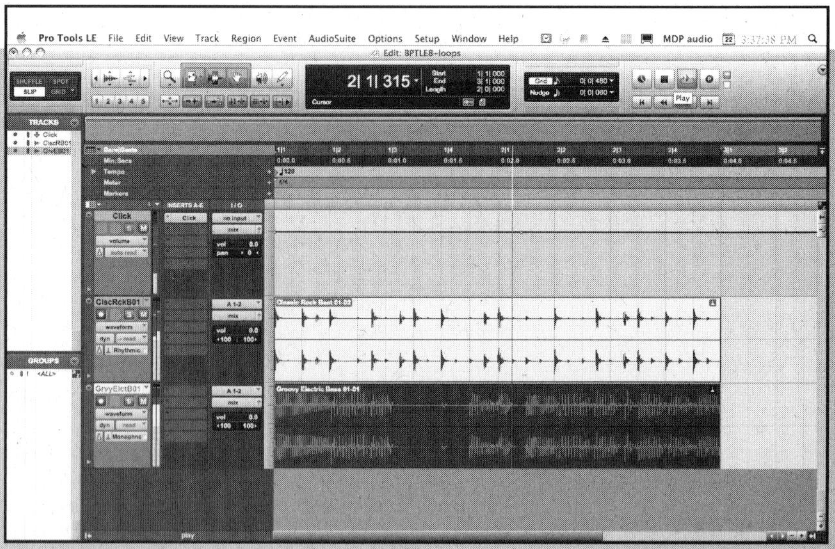

▲ ***Fig. 35: Two loops with different tempos are conforming to match the song tempo.***

Recording Basics

When recording vocals, guitars, or keyboards, your audio device will need to be set up correctly. Set the inputs of your audio device to line live when recording keyboards or guitar/bass amp emulator boxes like Line 6. Set your inputs to mic level for recording vocals, drums, percussion, or live guitar/bass cabinets. The recording levels in the digital world don't need to be extra hot. In the days of analog tape recording, you would sometimes push the input levels higher than normal to get a certain sound, but with modern computer-based recording, digital distortion sounds just plain ugly. When your inputs are all connected, check your levels. The peak of your levels should be around -10db on your readout. If you have your recording settings at 24 bit @ 48K, you're going to have plenty of headroom.

Sometimes after recording a passage, there may be a couple of measures that need to be fixed. This is where the terms punch in and punch out come from. We want to fix a portion of the track but leave the rest intact. Let's look at two ways of doing this.

In both of these examples, the original audio, or the portion you are fixing, is never erased, but only replaced. So if you get lost in what you are doing, you can always go back to the original and start over. That is the real beauty of digital recording.

The first example is called Quick Punch in Pro Tools. To activate Quick Punch go under Options in the main menu and choose Quick Punch. There should be a letter P in the Record icon at the top right hand of the Edit window. Put your track into record mode by pressing the Track Record Enable button that is just under the track name on the left side. It will turn red. Press the spacebar or Play button. Press the main Record button at measure two and press it again around measure three. You will see where it punched in and out.

▲ *Fig. 36: Quick Punch*

Now this time, record a vocal. Do something short for now so you can get the idea of punching in and out. After you have finished the first pass go back and punch in and out, but sing something different at the point where you punch. When you're done, playback your track with the replaced audio to hear the difference.

The second approach is to record several passes of the same section to get a perfect performance. To do this we need to set up a few things. Go up to Pro Tools LE in the main menu, then Preferences, choose Operations from the tabs, and then click on Automatically Create New Playlists When Loop Recording.

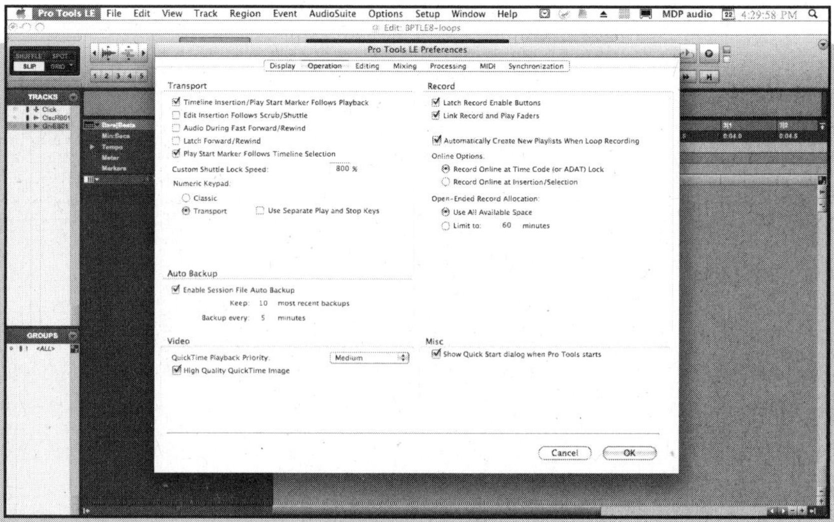

▲ ***Fig. 37: This option must be checked to enable Loop Recording.***

Close this window, put your track in record mode, and record a four- or eight-bar vocal or instrumental piece. Next, let's put the Edit window in Grid mode. In this mode, regions will snap to the value that the Grid is set to, such as quarter notes or multiple bars. You will also be able to see the beat division markers, and the selection tool will select at the same value. There are four boxes in top left-hand corner that control which mode the Edit window will be in. For now, click on Grid and hold to select Absolute. On the other side, you will see the word Grid in neon green. If it's not selected, click on it so it turns green. The note icon next to it is where you select the note or bar division amount to which the regions will adhere. When you make selections with your cursor or move regions around, they will move at the selected grid value.

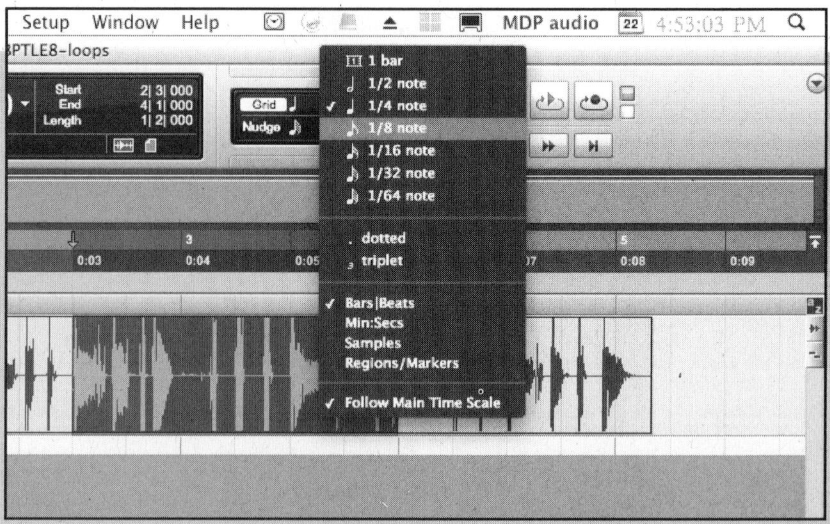

▲ ***Fig. 38: The value set here affects movement of the regions on the Grid.***

Let's fix measure three. Go up to Options in the main menu and select Loop Record. Loop Playback should still be enabled. Click on the Record icon, and it will start to flash. Use your cursor to select the punch in and punch out points. If you're punching in at measure three, start at measure two to give yourself a count off to know where you are. Set your punch out point a little afterwards also. Hit the Play button. Now, every time it loops, you can record a new take. When you are finished, click Stop. Go to the box in the track where it says waveform. Click and hold, and then select Playlists. You should see several regions of what you just recorded in loop record. They will be sequentially numbered and color coded.

▲ ***Fig. 39: The perfect vocal is assembled from multiple takes.***

You might see spaces where there's not any waveform, and the punch in and out points may look funny. No worries. In the next chapter, we will discuss editing, and you will learn how to select your best performances and clean up your Edit page.

CHAPTER 7 THE EDITING TOOLBOX

Pro Tools has always been the default audio DAW in studios around the world. You will probably find a version of Pro Tools anywhere you go. Even if it's not the primary software being utilized in a studio (but most of the time it is) you'll find it is a part of almost every recording package in the studio for hire business. The reason for this is that once you learn the basics and the key commands, you will feel comfortable in whatever situation you find yourself in. No learning curve in figuring out another DAW. No reading a manual to find how to work a digital tape or hard disk machine. Other reasons are the editing capabilities and the editing tools. Here's a quick look into some of the resources available to you.

Audio Editing

Now let's take the last example and make a final track out of the four takes. When you are listening to your take you are always hearing what is on the top track. In the example the takes are numbered as 01, 02, 03, and 04. To hear any of the other takes, click on the S solo button under the track name. The button will turn yellow. Highlight the track, click play and you will hear the new take.

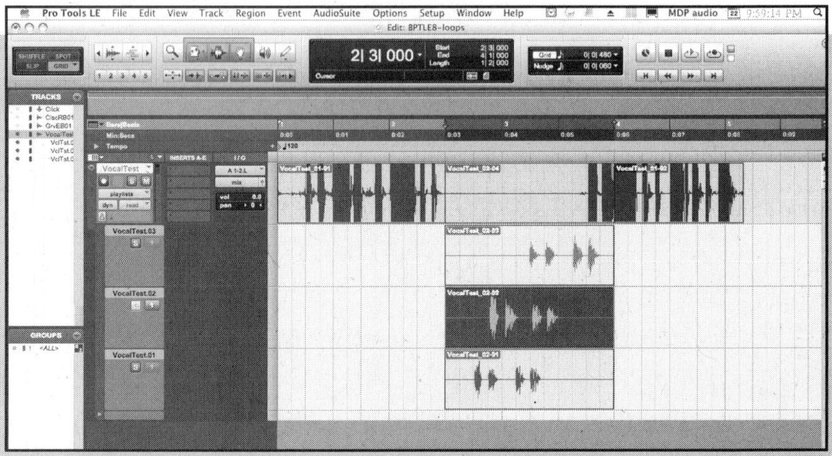

▲ ***Fig. 40: Use the Solo button to hear each playlist take.***

Once you find the take you like the best, click the arrow that is pointing up that is to the right of the S button and the take will be inserted into the track.

Click on the S button to turn off solo and then go up and click on playlist and choose waveform. The track will close and you will have your new take.

The original audio and all the takes are still there. They have not been erased. All that has happened is that the regions have been manipulated to start and end in different places.

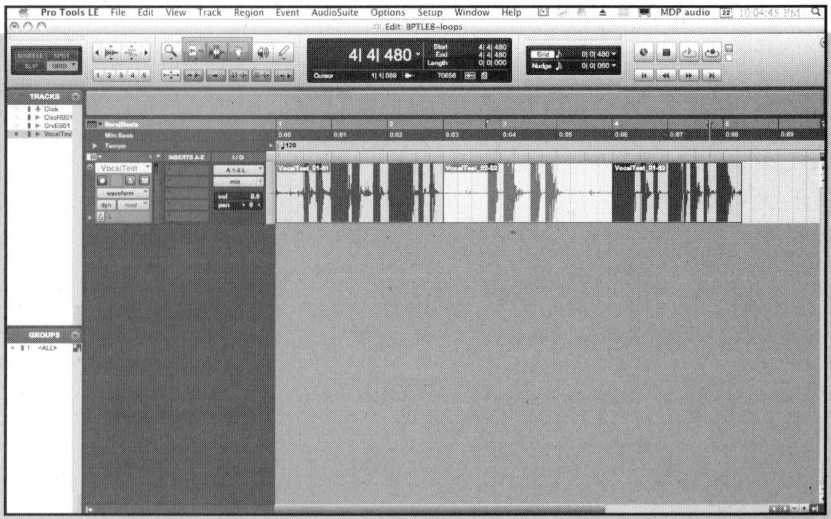

▲ ***Fig. 41: The perfect take is inserted into the master track.***

Display Tools

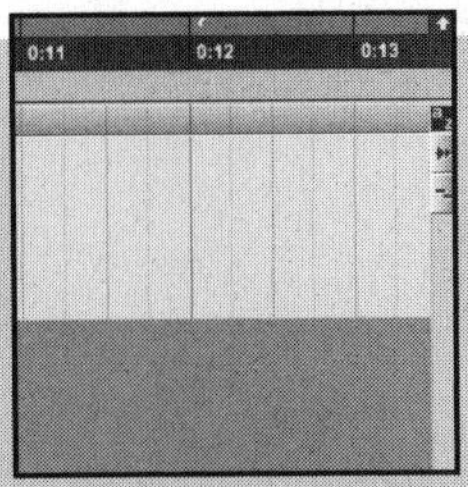

▲ *Fig. 42: Audio MIDI Zoom.*

Let's widen the track out so we can really see how the tools work. First, a couple of display tools. To the right you will see a box with an a and z in it, a box with a little audio waveform, and another box with a couple of dash looking figures which in Pro Tools world means MIDI. The bottom to boxes are zoom controls, one for audio and one for MIDI. The top of each box zooms and the bottom of each box zooms down. Those very same controls are right beside the Edit mode buttons (Grid, Slip) if they are selected in the Edit Window Menu.

▲ *Fig. 43: Mode Smart Tool Zoom*

The little box with the a and z in it is the Commands Keyboard Focus selector. When selected in the Tracks pane in the Edit window or in the Notes pane of any MIDI Editor window, this provides a wide range of single key shortcuts from the computer keyboard for editing and playing. The front most Edit or MIDI Editor window always receives Commands Keyboard Focus when it is enabled. With Commands Keyboard Focus disabled, you can still access any of its key shortcuts by pressing the Start key (Windows) or Control (Mac) along with the key. For a complete list of Commands Keyboard Focus shortcuts, see the Shortcuts Guide in your installation materials.

We touched on the Edit mode buttons in the last chapter but there is a little more to know because of how it related to the selected tool. There are four selections in the box located at the top left hand corner of the Edit window. The Edit mode affects the movement and placement of audio and MIDI regions (and MIDI notes), how commands like Copy and Paste function, and also how the various Edit tools (Trim, Selector, Grabber, and Pencil tools) work.

In Grid mode, regions and MIDI notes that are moved, trimmed or inserted "snap" to the currently selected Grid value, or to precise increments on a user-definable time grid. The definable grid is on the other side of the counter. The word Grid is next to a note icon. Clicking on the icon opens a menu of the divisions you can select from.

In Slip mode, regions can be moved freely within a track or to other tracks. In this mode, it is possible to place a region so that there is space between it and other regions in a track. When the track is played back, this space is silent. It is also possible to move a region so that it overlaps or completely covers another region.

Use Spot mode to place regions at precise locations. When Spot mode is enabled, Pro Tools asks you to specify a destination location when a region is dragged from the Region List.

In Shuffle mode, you can move, trim, delete, cut, or paste regions freely within a track or to other tracks, but their movement is constrained by other regions. That is, if you place several regions in a track, they automatically snap to each other. You can then "shuffle" their order, but you cannot separate them from each other and you cannot make them overlap as in Slip mode. However, if there is silence between existing regions, and the regions are shuffled, the silence is maintained, and not removed. In Shuffle mode, adding another region to the beginning of a track moves all subsequent regions to the right (later in time) by the length of the added region. When using any of the Trimmer tools in Shuffle mode, changing a region's start or end point automatically moves any subsequent regions as necessary.

▲ ***Fig. 44: A region is a segment of audio, MIDI, or video data.***

The Regions list (Fig. 44) gives you a visual of all the audio that is being used in this session. To see the list, click on the regions hide and show selector.

Clicking on it opens the list (Fig. 45). If you need to make it wider place your cursor on the left side border. It will turn into a solid bar with arrows pointing out on each side, which means you can slide the border back and forth. Click on the triangle on the right side of the word Regions and it will open a menu list of all the functions you can apply to the regions in the list. Consult the guide for all you can do here.

▲ ***Fig. 45: Region List Options***

The upside down triangle at the top right-hand corner is the Edit Window Menu selector. Clicking on it will give a list of the functions you do and do not want displayed in the top of the Edit window (Fig. 46).

▲ ***Fig. 46: Customize how your display looks with these options.***

Editing Tools

Take a look at the top display where you see the magnifying glass on one side and the pencil on the other. The three tools in middle have a bar going across the top of them. Clicking on it turns it blue. This is called the Smart tool because when you place your cursor over a region or regions, and slowly move it around you will see the cursor turn into different tools. Let's go through the tools.

Click and hold on the Magnifying tool. The first selection leaves the tool as the cursor until you change it. The second selection is called Single because after you zoom a selection it automatically goes back to the previous tool.

Click and hold on the next tool, which is the trimmer tool. There are three selections: *Standard* for basic trimming, *TCE* Time Compression and Expansion, which is a little advanced for this example (consult your Pro Tools Reference Guide when you're ready), and the *Loop* selection.

Use this tool on your favorite drumbeat by selecting the end of the region, and then holding and dragging to the right for as many measures as you need. The grid selection affects this tool. Sometimes you will want to use Slip mode, which uses no constraint when moving the borders, but most of the time Grid mode will work.

The next tool is the selector tool. As you move across tracks and regions you will see how this tool works. It is also Grid dependent.

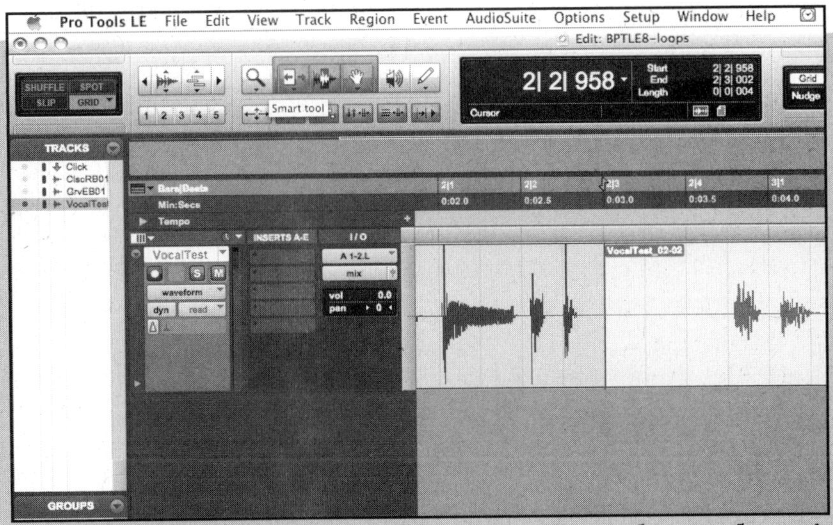

▲ ***Fig. 47: The smart tool changes into other tools as it moves across a region.***

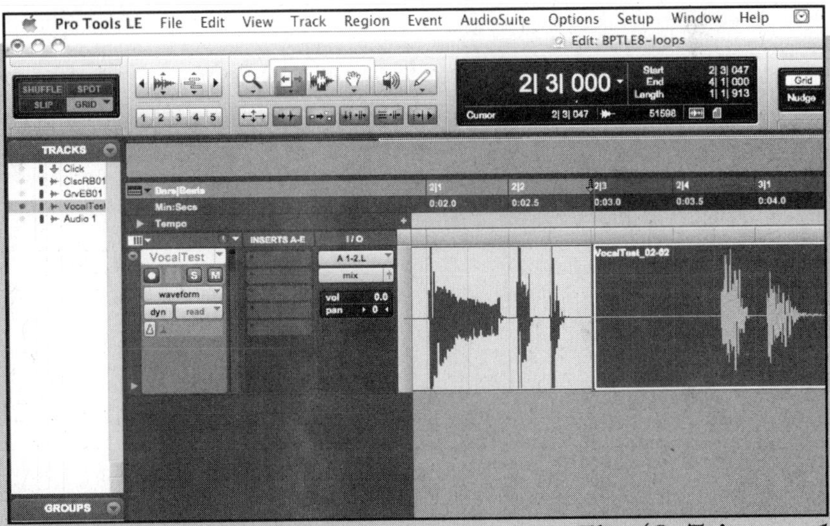

▲ ***Fig. 48: Trimmer 1***

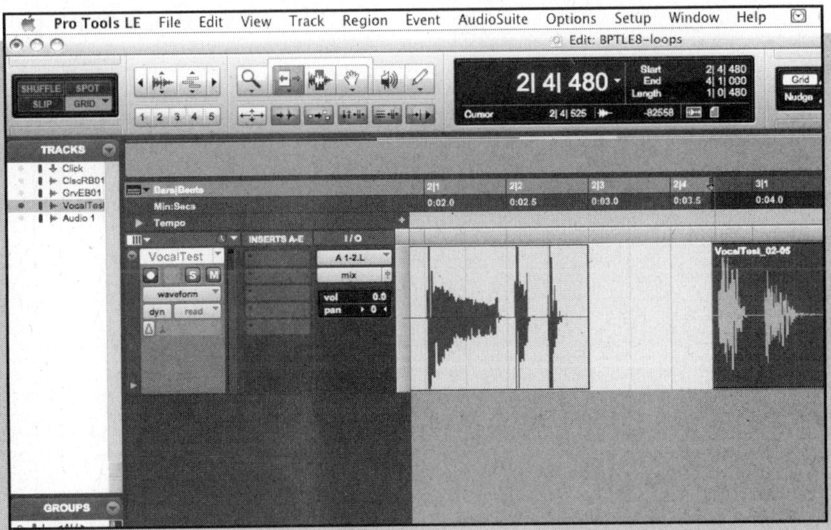

▲ ***Fig. 49: Trimmer 2***

The icon of the hand is the Grabber tool. It has three selections: *Time* Selects an entire region in a track. *Separation* cuts and paste a selection within a region to be place in another track. *Object* selects regions from different tracks at the same time.

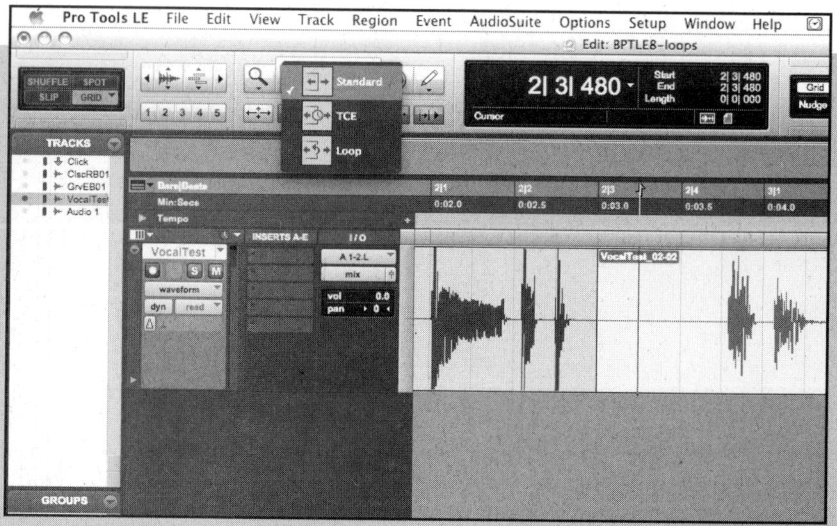

▲ ***Fig. 50: Grabber Tool***

The Scrubber tool lets you "scrub" up to two tracks of audio in the Edit Window. Scrubbing is a technique that originated in tape editing, where the tape was rocked back and forth past the play head at slower than normal speeds to find a particular location (usually for cutting and splicing). While viewing an audio waveform in Pro Tools can be helpful in visually finding an edit point, sometimes a waveform display (because of its sonic characteristics) may not reveal the desired spot in the audio material. By scrubbing back and forth in Pro Tools, you can listen and locate an exact edit point.

The Pencil tool lets you draw audio waveforms (at the sample level), tempo changes, MIDI data, and automation.

All of these tools can be used more extensively than what is shown here. Get into the manuals and guides and find out all the cool stuff you can do with these tools.

As stated before, the new audio files that we recorded did not erase any of the original audio but just replaced it with the new audio. Using a couple of tools we can fix our original track that we punched into.

As you can see there is a big gap in the front of the new take that was inserted. This was take #2 and the 05 means there are five versions of this region. Click on the Standard Trimmer tool and select the new take region (Fig. 51).

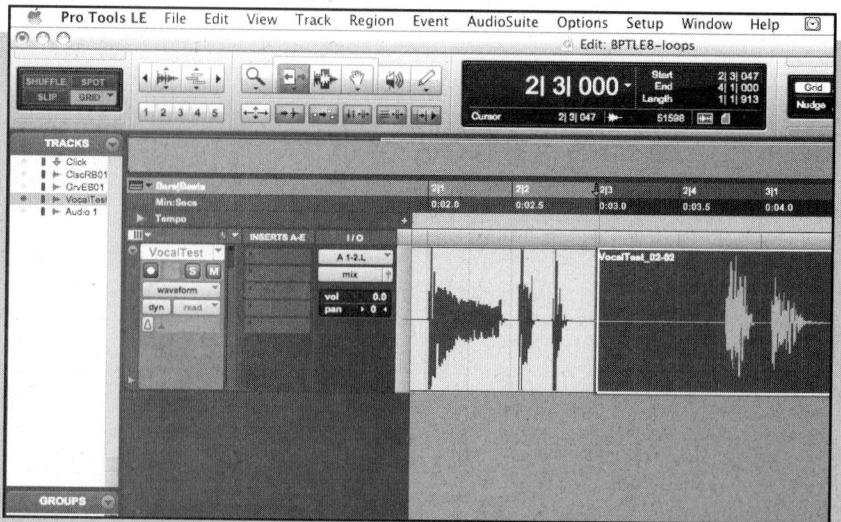

▲ ***Fig. 51: Select a region with the Standard Trimmer tool.***

Place the cursor at the left border of the new take region until the cursor is pointing to the right. Click, hold, and drag to the right. It will make this region shorter (Fig. 52).

▲ ***Fig. 52: Drag the selected region to make it shorter.***

Place the cursor on the right border of original take region that is to the left of the new take region until the pointers of the trimmer tool are pointing to the left. Click, hold, and drag to the right. You will see the original take waveform starting to reveal itself as this region gets longer. Pull the border over until it meets the left border of the new take region (Fig. 53).

▲ ***Fig. 53: Expand the region to the left to reveal the original take.***

Click on the smart tool and place your cursor at the bottom of where the two regions meet. The cursor will look like a box. This tool is the crossfade tool. It helps clean up the transitions between regions. Click, hold, and pull the mouse to the right or the left. A box with an X in it will get larger the farther you pull it to the right or left. Pull the box with the X in it really wide, so can you hear what the X-marked cross-fade does between the two regions, then shrink it back by pulling the box the other way and you'll understand how the cross-fade impacts the audio file based on its size.(Fig 54).

▲ ***Fig. 54: Use the Crossfade feature to clean up the transition.***

These examples of editing your audio just barley touch the first level of what Pro Tools can do. To really grasp the power of this program will take some patience as you read all the materials, but as you go little deeper into it you will unlock your creative potential.

We've been learning the basics of editing on one track. Let's work on some multiple tracks and find out a little more about editing audio in Pro Tools LE.

CHAPTER 8 MORE ABOUT AUDIO EDITING

In the real world of recording studios, time is a big issue. An engineer who knows how to efficiently navigate a DAW is invaluable. Knowing how to do complex tasks on multiple files in a small amount of time is the mark of a true professional. Let's look at how some of the tools we have been talking about can be applied on a larger scale.

Group Editing

This chapter will make more sense if you have a multiple-file session at your disposal to experiment with the techniques as they are discussed. If you don't, please watch the DVD and/or look at the examples in this book to understand the basics of group editing.

The first thing that is obvious about group editing is that there has to be a group! Let's look at an example of a drum session with 17 tracks. Our goal is to group the drums together so edits applied to one track apply to all of them. Why do I want to edit all of them together?

In a drum recording like the one in this example, all the mics are in close proximity to each other. If you were to solo the snare mic, you would hear the rest of the drum kit. They will be much softer than the snare, but still too prominent to ignore. Likewise, if you solo the overhead mics, you would hear the rest of the kit in addition to the cymbals. So if there was a late hit on a snare beat and you moved just the snare track up a little bit in time, you would hear the rest of the kit, which is present on the snare mic, jump out ahead of the other 16 tracks because of "bleed through." That's the name given to sounds that are unintentionally recorded because of their proximity to another microphone. The snare drum, kick, toms, and the hi-hat "bleed through" into the overhead mics, which are recorded to the overhead tracks because they are present in the same room as the cymbals.

So, instead of moving one track enough to correct the timing error, we need to group the tracks and make the same edit on all of them.

First, click on the name of your first track.

▲ ***Fig. 55: Select the first track of the group.***

Then, shift click on the last track you want to be in the group. Now all the tracks in between those two should be highlighted.

At the bottom left-hand corner, you will see two icons, both resembling the regions list Show and Hide selector. The one with the arrow pointing up is the MIDI Pane Show and Hide selector. We will discuss MIDI in a different chapter. The one with the arrow pointing to the right is the Tracks and Groups List Show and Hide selector. Click on it to show the Group list.

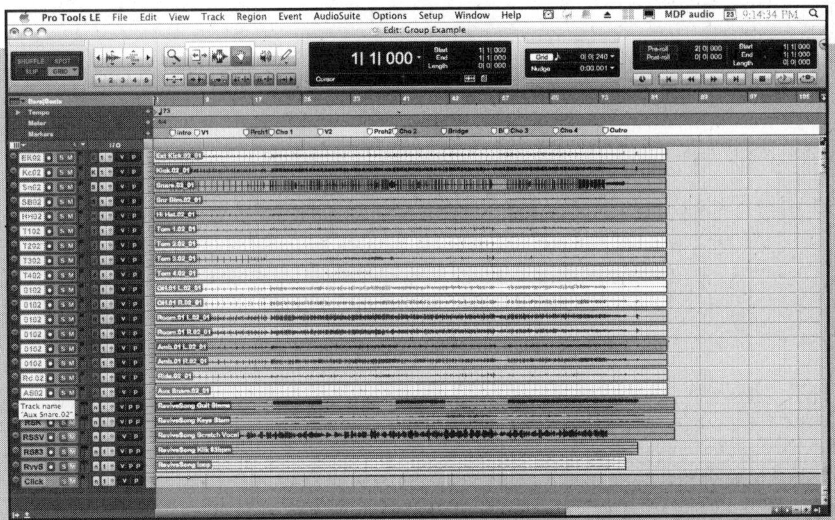

▲ ***Fig. 56: Shift click on the last track to select all tracks in between.***

Now you will see all the tracks you have selected highlighted in dark gray in the Tracks list. To the right of the word Groups, click on the triangle. From the menu choose New Group, and a Group window will open.

▲ ***Fig. 57: Select New Group.***

Select the tracks that you want to be grouped, name the group, and choose which functions you want the group to respond to when you edit one of the tracks of the group.

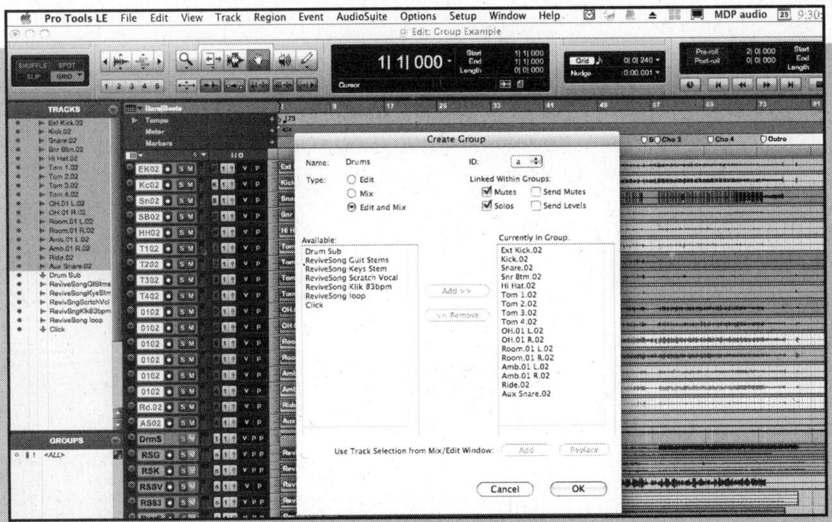

▲ ***Fig. 58: Set options for the new group.***

Close the window and choose the Grabber tool. Click on any of the tracks, and the whole group will highlight. You will see your group name in the Groups list (Fig. 59).

Suppose you are hearing a rhythm problem in the drums and it's because a kick drum is late. We now know that we can't move the kick track by itself because of the bleed through of the other drums on its track. We need to edit all the drums at the same time.

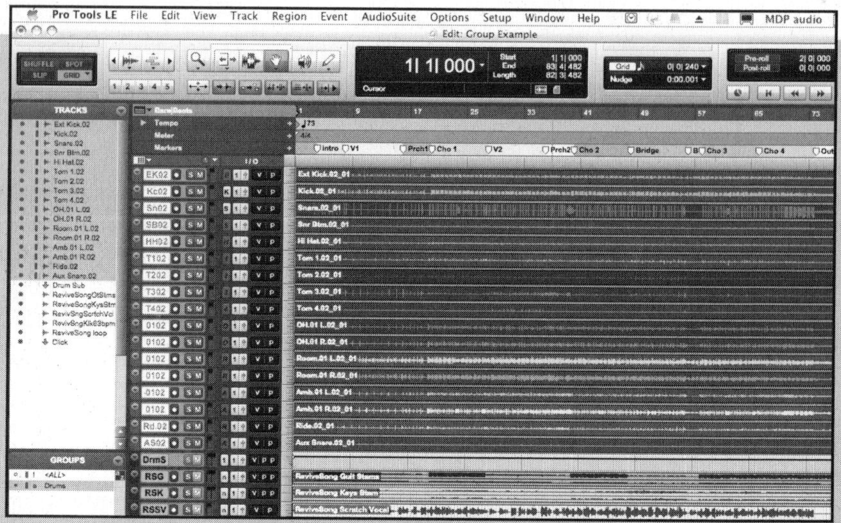

▲ *Fig. 59: The new group appears in the Groups list.*

As we listen down to the track, we find the culprit and look to see at what measure the problem occurs. In the example, we want to fix the kick track on the downbeat of measure 10. We need to make a cut across all the tracks at this point.

To cut a region or regions, Pro Tools has a function called Separate Region. You can use it by going under Edit in the main menu, Separate Region, and then selecting At Selection. An easier way to do it is to use the key command Apple E (Fig. 60).

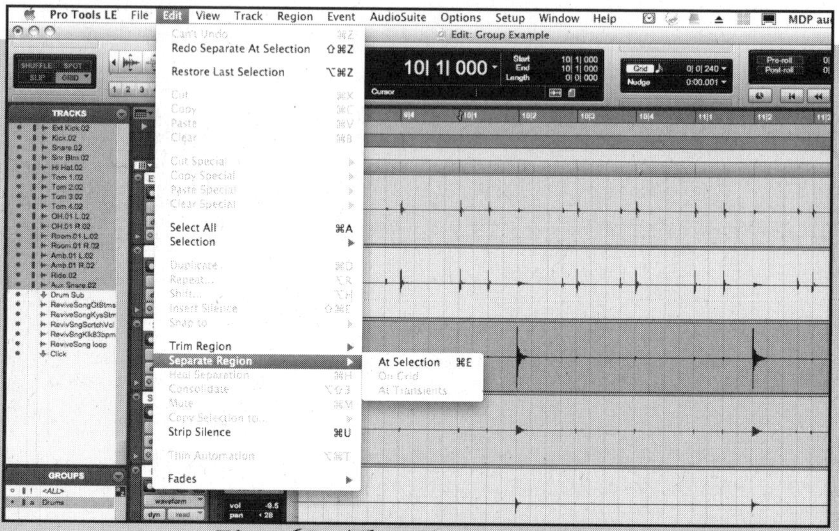

▲ *Fig. 60: The Separate Regions command works on a single track or multiple tracks. Apple E is the Key Command.*

Take the Selector tool and click on measure 10. Make sure you are in Grid mode so that the selector moves at a precise division. You want to cut exactly at measure 10. As soon as you see you are at measure 10, use the Apple E command and you will see a line go across all your grouped tracks. You now have one set of regions on the left side of the cut and one set of regions on the right side. You will also see that the regions to the right of the separation have a new name.

▲ *Fig. 61: Drum tracks are divided into separate regions.*

All track names start out with the format "name01" (where "name" is the actual name of the track), and they stay that way until there is a separation performed on that region. Now there are two regions, so the second will be called "name02".

Check to see what value your Grid division is set at. Choose a 16th note.

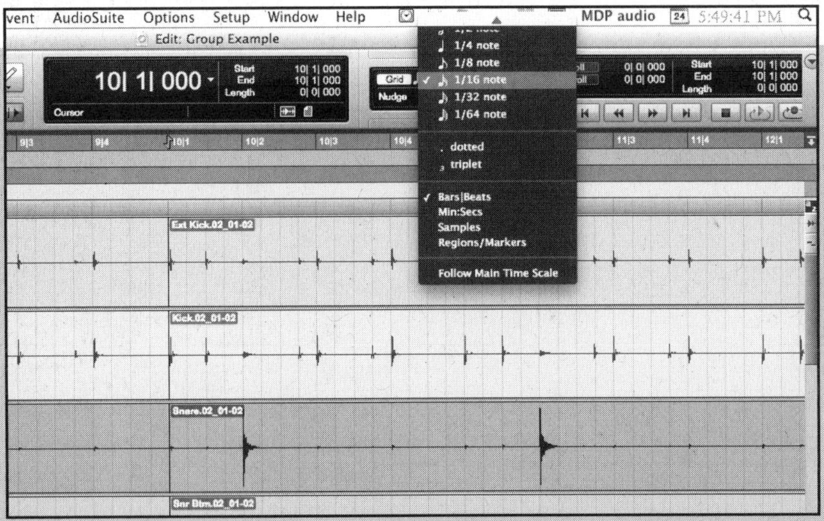

▲ ***Fig. 62: Select 16th from Grid.***

We want to cut just a small part of the track, so move the Selector tool over to the next 16th note on the grid. Use the Apple E command. Now you have a small section that has been separated from the rest of the tracks.

▲ ***Fig. 63: A 16th-note region has been selected.***

Go up to the Edit mode buttons and choose Slip. This mode is for moving items "freestyle." It's not constrained to any values, which is very useful when fixing small areas where there are rhythm problems. Use the Grabber tool to select the small section of regions that you are going to move. Click, hold, and pull your mouse to the left just a small amount. You're trying to get the kick to play a little bit earlier, so you may have to try a few times until it sounds right.

▲ ***Fig. 64: Using Slip Mode and listening several times to your edit will help you find the correct placement.***

Once you're satisfied with the edit, select the Smart tool and put your cursor on the right edge of the small set of regions. Move the cursor until it becomes the Trimmer tool. Click, hold and pull the mouse back to the right until it meets with the 3rd section of regions (Figs. 65 and 66).

▲ ***Fig. 65: Select the right edge of the region with the Trimmer tool.***

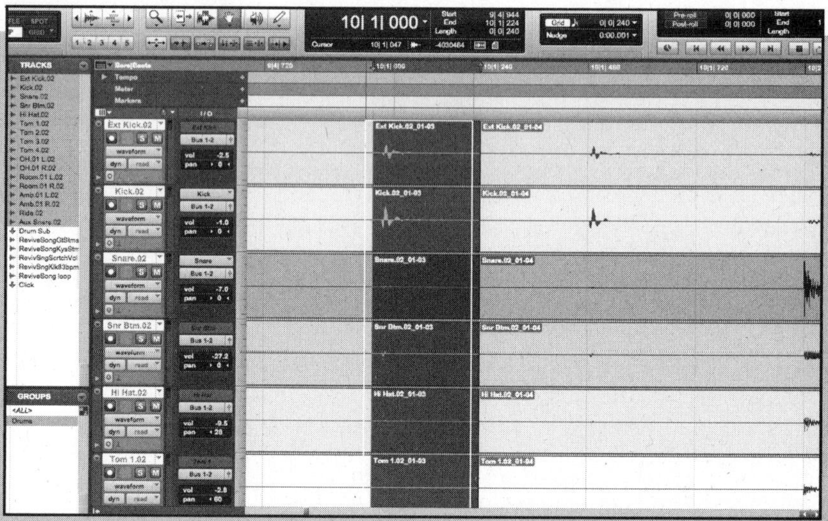

▲ ***Fig. 66: Drag the region to the right until it meets the adjacent region.***

With the Smart tool still selected, place the cursor at the bottom of one of the tracks where the last two regions meet until the cursor turns into the Crossfade tool. Click, hold, and pull to the left or right to make your crossfade.

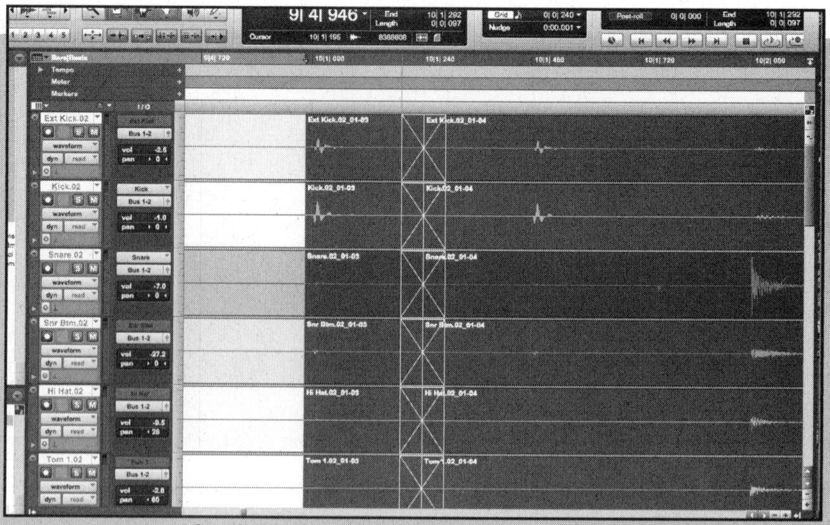

▲ ***Fig. 67: Use the Crossfade tool to create a smooth transition between regions.***

Since these tracks are grouped, the same crossfade will be placed on each track (Fig. 68).

When you are in Grid mode and you are moving regions, there are two selections you can make. The first selection is Absolute, which means when you move the region, it moves according to the increments selected in the Grid Value selector. If the cut is before the downbeat of beat one, and you move it to the next beat, it will place the cut at beat two. In Relative mode, Pro Tools retains the location of the cut relative to the beat and then moves it at the Grid value. These two selections will help you find that perfect edit and crossfade.

▲ ***Fig. 68: The crossfade is applied to each track in the group.***

Be Organized

Digital audio editing is an amazing development. It's not only a great technical tool, but I have also found it to be a creative tool I can use when I am composing music. However, as you cut, paste, and move regions, the Edit page will become quite scrambled looking. We are adding MIDI to the picture in the next chapter, so it's going to get an even "busier" look on your monitor. That's why it's important to do a few secretarial operations on your Edit page so that when you open up a session you'll know exactly what you are looking at.

Color-coding is used in all types of business for organizing massive amounts of information, and Pro Tools is no exception. In the example above, all of the tracks are colored blue. Double click on one of the blue areas, and a color palette will pop up (Fig. 69).

There, you can choose the color you want and tweak it with saturation and brightness adjustment faders. Play around with the controls and release your inner visual artist.

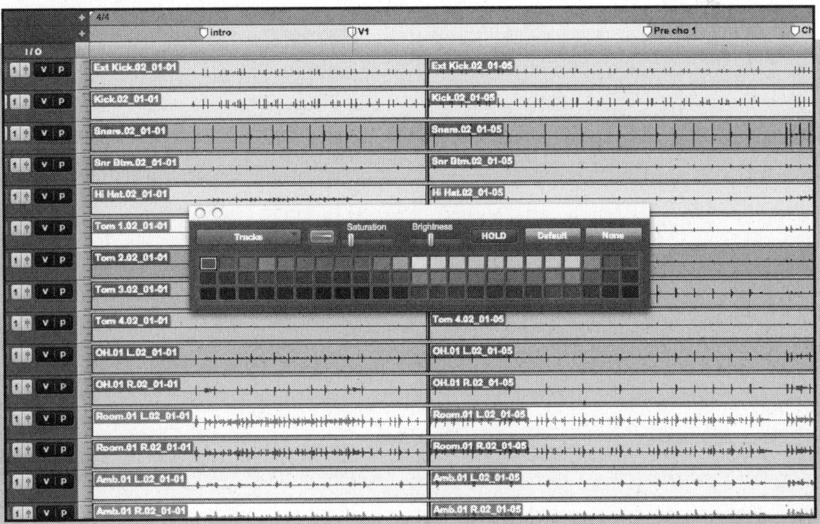

▲ ***Fig. 69: Color Palette popup***

Click on the menu and you can choose to color-code just about anything.

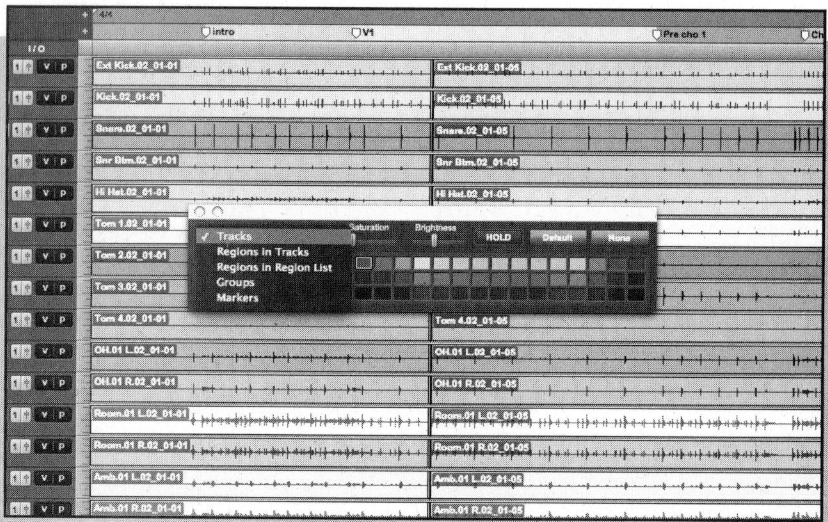

▲ ***Fig. 69: You can color-code just about anything!***

In the example on the right, all the edits that have been made on our grouped drums are color-coded.

▲ ***Fig. 70: The drum edits have been color-coded.***

You can see how this can take a crazy (and maybe ugly in some cases), mixed-up looking bunch of tracks and regions, and give them some kind orderly appearance.

The next thing you can do to clean up the Edit page is called Consolidation. All that means is once you are happy with a track that you have done multiple edits to, and you have all your crossfades perfected, you can take all those regions and turn them into one continuous new audio file. Doing this gets rid of all the little cuts, edits, and crossfade boxes and makes one clean file. It's very easy to do, and you can do it to one or multiple files. In our example, we will use the Selector tool to select a stereo electric guitar track made up of different takes. You must be sure that your selection starts at zero and goes to the end of the last file.

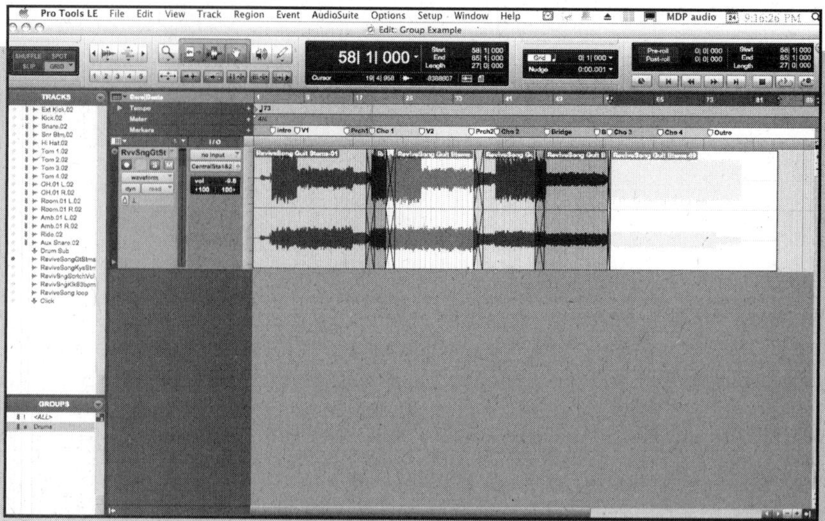

▲ ***Fig. 71: Select multiple regions to consolidate.***

Go under Edit in the main menu and choose Consolidate.

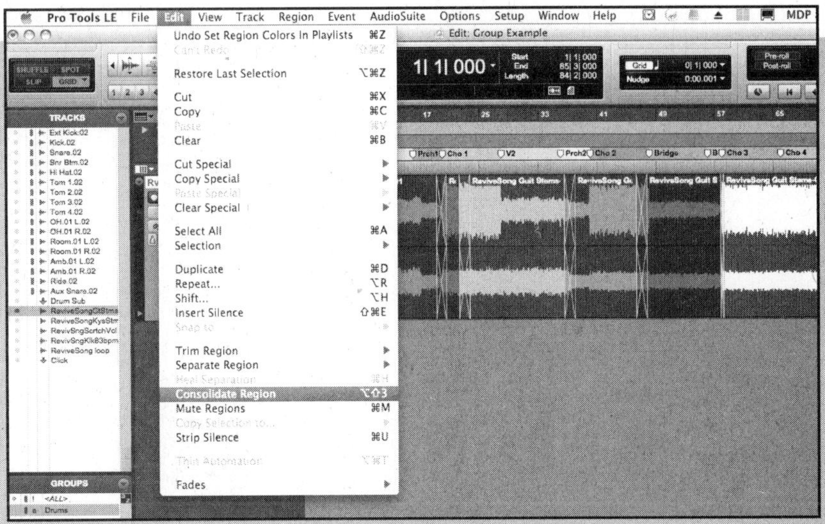

▲ *Fig. 72: Choose the Consolidate command.*

You'll see a message about processing. The new file is being stored in the same folder as the rest of your audio.

▲ *Fig. 73: A popup windows shows the progress of the Consolidation process.*

Once it is finished you will be left with one stereo file ready for mix, export, or storage (Fig. 74).

You can apply this process to as many files as you want at the same time. Just use the Selector tool and click and hold while you drag across the tracks that you want to consolidate, being sure to drag to the beginning of the session.

Pro Tools LE 8 not only is a monster when it comes to audio editing, but it also has a brand-spanking-new updated MIDI package too! The next chapter will get into how to record and edit MIDI for your projects and compositions.

▲ *Fig. 74: The result is a single consolidated file.*

CHAPTER 9 MIDI—A BRAND NEW LOOK

The MIDI capabilities of Pro Tools have never enjoyed a very good reputation compared with other DAW's on the market. As a composer, I found working with MIDI in Pro Tools not to be very intuitive or inspiring. Many DAW's over the past few years have been rolling out not only great MIDI sequencing but great software instrument plug-ins also.

Well… all of that has changed with Pro Tools LE 8. Digidesign has developed some amazing instrument plug-ins and plug-in libraries that rival any other software program out there. Way to go, Digidesign!

Recording MIDI

Create a new session and name it MIDI or some other descriptive label. Use this session for a while to practice. Next, determine what you want your tempo to be. You can set the tempo by selecting the Event menu and then choosing Tempo Operations, or by double clicking the red flag on the tempo bar. This example is set for 120 bpm. Next let's pull up the Transport window so we can see it. It's located under Window in the main menu. You can see there are other windows you can reveal, but for now just choose Transport.

Next, let's create a click track and an Instrument track named Drums.

▲ *Fig. 75: Create a click track and a drum track.*

As always, save your session every once in a while, even if you have auto backup enabled. In the example, there is a little white box with stripes next to a triangle on the top left-hand corner called the Edit Window View selector. Clicking on this triangle allows you to view the different configurations of inserts and input/output selections in your project. You can view as little or as much detail as you want. For this example, select the Instrument view and the Inserts A-E view.

▲ *Fig. 76: The Edit Window View selector*

Click on the Instrument view button to confirm that you are sending and receiving on the right MIDI input and output. Click on the Insert A slot, scroll over to BFD Lite, and click on it.

▲ *Fig. 77: Select the BFD Lite insert.*

Go to your MIDI keyboard and play a few notes to confirm you are triggering the BFD plug-in.

▲ *Fig. 78: Triggering the BFD Lite Plugin.*

MIDI Merge

We are going to show a couple of ways to record MIDI into Pro Tools LE. The first way is called MIDI merge. A loop is set up to record over and over, and each time the loop repeats, a new pass of MIDI is added to the original. This method of MIDI recording is used in drum sequencing. Say you want the first verse of a song you're working on to be four bars in length and you want the drums to play a very simple pattern. Let's look at how how you accomplish this goal.

We need to set up the software for MIDI merge recording. First, turn off Loop Recording. Remember where that is? We used it when we were doing multiple passes of audio. It's under Options in the main menu. MIDI merge will not work with Loop Recording on. While you're in the Options menu, make sure Loop Playback is on. There will be a line going around in a circle with an arrow on one end inside the Transport window Play button.

On the Transport window, click on the MIDI merge button, which is in between the metronome icon and the conductor icon.

▲ ***Fig. 79: MIDI Merge is for recording multiple passes of a MIDI instrument in Loop Record.***

Select Absolute Grid for the Edit mode and use a one bar division. Be sure and click on the green Grid button on the right so that you will see your divisions on the Edit page. Take the Selector tool and starting from measure one, click, hold, and drag to the end of measure six. The reason for this is so you will have one bar of rest to prepare for each subsequent pass. This is your loop. Arm the track, then press the Record button on the transport, and it will begin to flash.

When you're ready to record, hit the Play button. Give yourself one bar of click and then start playing on measure two. Play a kick pattern. At the end of bar six, it will loop back to measure one. Let it go for one bar and play a snare pattern. On the next pass, play a hi-hat pattern. When you're done, click Stop. Take the track and transport out of record mode. The region you have been recording will now have a bunch of dots and dash looking symbols representing MIDI data.

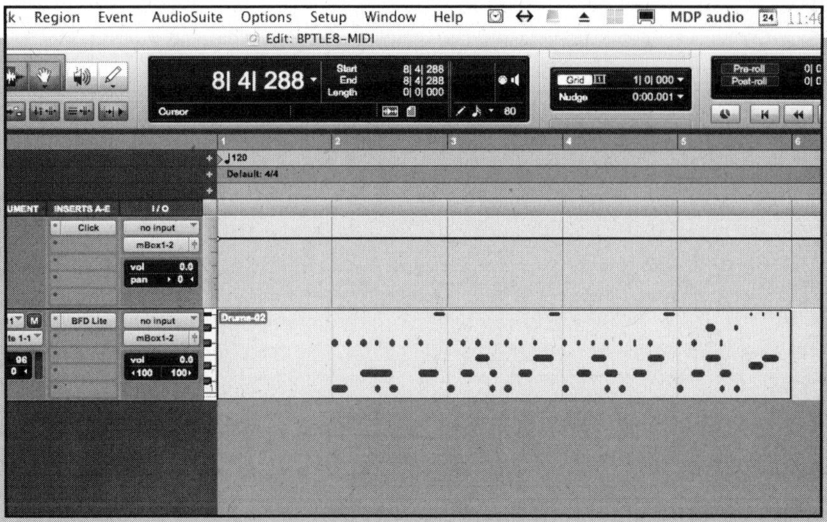

▲ ***Fig. 80: After recording a MIDI Merge session with a drum plug-in, this is what the region will look like.***

With the Selector tool and the Grid mode still set on one bar, select measures two through six and hit Play. The performance may not sound very tight, so right click on the region and you will see a menu. Near the bottom of the menu, select Events, and a sub menu will come up.

▲ ***Fig. 81: Right clicking on the region will bring up a menu for all kinds of functions.***

Choose Quantize from that menu. The Quantize selection snaps the beginning of notes or data selected to the defined quantize value. In this example, since we have selected the entire region, all notes will quantized to the sixteenth note value.

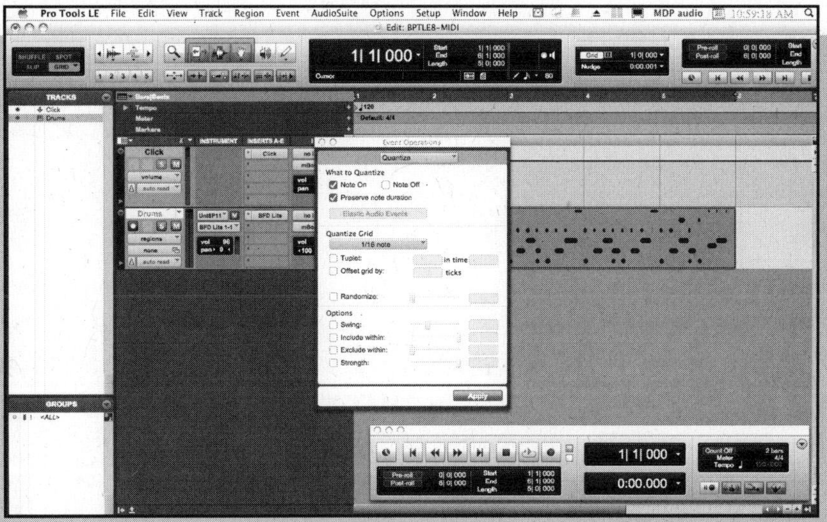

▲ ***Fig. 82: Quantize the region to the 16th-note value.***

Click Apply, close the window and hit Play. Now the performance sounds tight.

There are other values to select from in the Events Window that can alter the behavior of notes and all kinds of MIDI information.

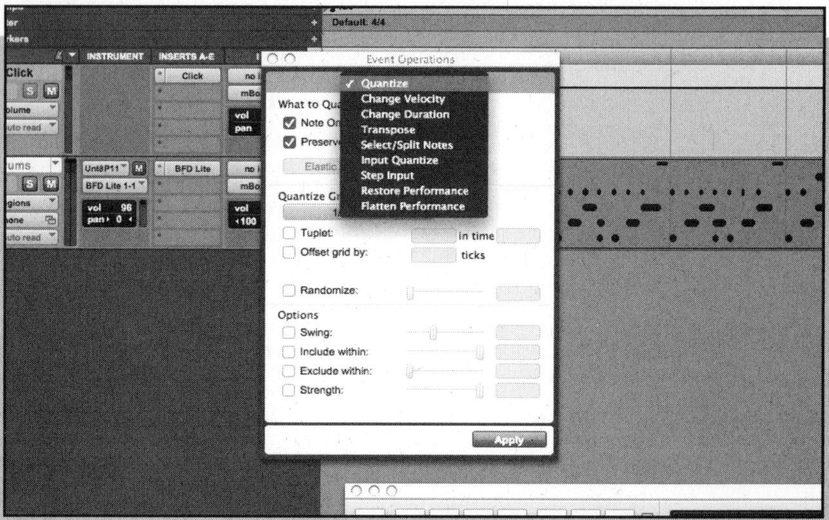

▲ ***Fig. 83: Quantizing notes can be as rigid or subtle as you want.***

Take this same drum pass and select some of the other choices in the Event Operations window menu, like velocity or duration, and see what kind different effects you can come up with. If you don't like what you have done, just use the universal Mac undo key command Apple Z and try again.

Replace Style MIDI Recording

The replace style of recording is very similar to multiple take audio recording we discussed earlier. There are some terminology differences, but it's basically the same idea.

First, turn off MIDI Merge on the Transport window. Go up and click on Options in the main menu and select Loop Recording. There will be a line going around in a circle with an arrow on one end inside the Transport window Record button.

Now, create a new stereo Instrument track and name it Piano.

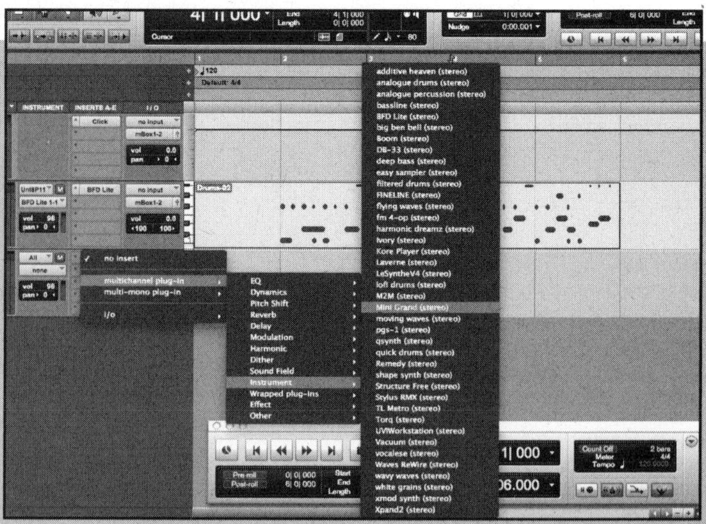

▲ ***Fig. 84: Create a new Instrument track named Piano.***

The Inserts A-E view is already engaged, so click on the first slot. Choose multichannel plug-in, Instrument, and then Mini Grand. The plug-in will take a few seconds to load the piano samples. A small red line will appear to show you it's in the loading process.

▲ ***Fig. 85: The Mini Grand instrument***

When the plug-in is fully loaded, check your MIDI inputs and outputs like we did on the drum track to make sure the plug-in is "seeing" your MIDI interface. Once you have confirmed that your piano is working, close the plug-in window. Use the Selector tool to highlight the same five bars like we did before. Arm your track (put it in record), click on the Record button in the Transport window, and it will start flashing.

▲ ***Fig. 86: The flashing Record button indicates the track is armed.***

You will be recording multiple passes but only seeing the last take on the Edit page. First, you'll be stacking performances on top of each other, and then after you are done recording, deciding which take or edits of takes you want to use.

When you hit Play, there will be a one-bar count off from bar one. Then you'll play from bars two through five. It will loop back to bar one, and you will get a one bar count again. This time, play something a little bit different, then do a 3rd pass, once again slightly modifying what you play. The reason for this is so you can hear the three different passes to give you an idea of how to use this recording option. After you have finished, open up the regions list, and you will see the piano regions you have recorded, which will be numbered in the sequence that you recorded them. Once you're finished recording, and there is a region in the piano track, right click on it to open up a menu. From the menu choose Matches. There you will see your piano takes listed, and you can choose any one of them you want. You can also choose from the regions list any one of the tracks, then click, hold, and drag the regions over to bar one.

▲ *Fig. 87: Select MIDI Matches.*

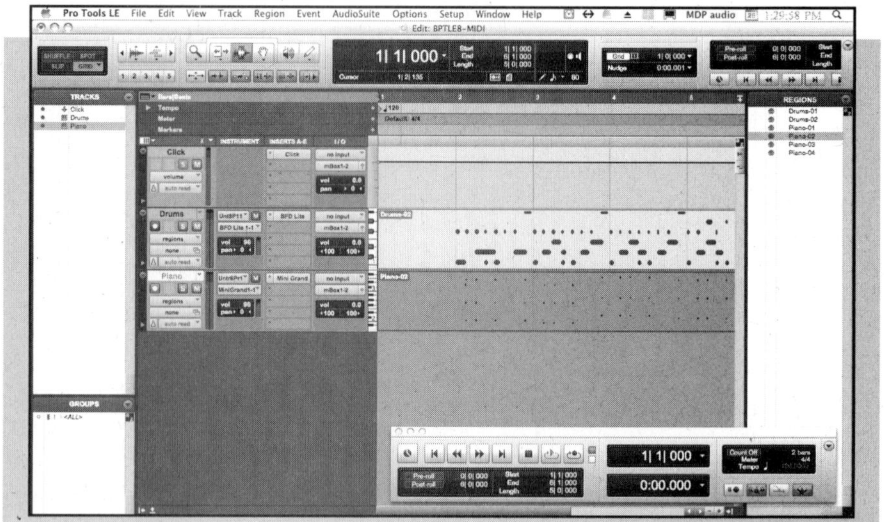

▲ *Fig. 88: Match 02 has been selected.*

MIDI and More

MIDI tracks can contain all kinds of information including velocity, duration, program changes, tempos, markers, and much more.

Markers and tempos are critical information, especially working with clients in other cities or countries. One big benefit of the digital audio age is the ability to share projects all over the world. Being able to send the technical information in MIDI files is a big time saver and keeps everyone synced up together.

In this example, you will be shown how to import a MIDI file that contains MIDI regions, markers, and tempo information into a blank session. Create a blank session. It will automatically have a tempo of 120 and a time signature of $\frac{4}{4}$.

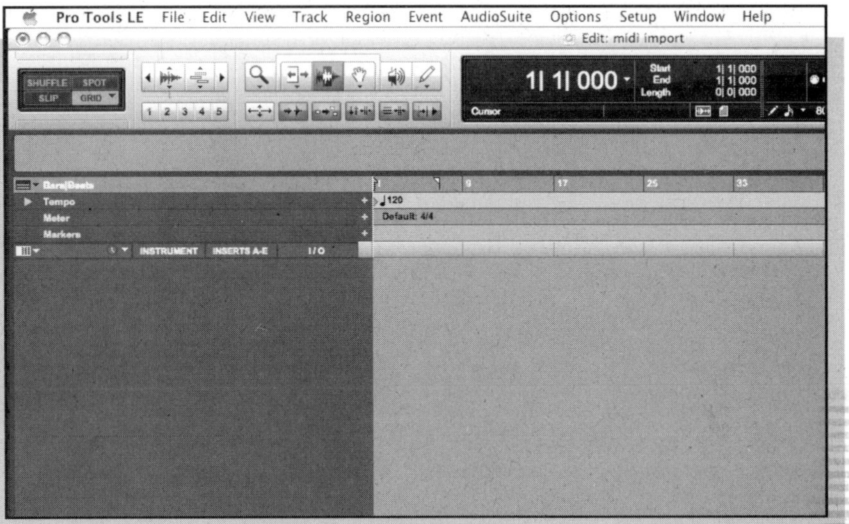

▲ ***Fig. 89: Create a blank session.***

To import a MIDI file, click on File in the main menu and place your cursor on the Import folder, and a menu of options will open. Choose MIDI and go to the hard drive and folder where the MIDI file is located.

▲ ***Fig. 90: Choose Import MIDI from the menu.***

Once you find it, double click on it. Choose the Options that you want imported, and in a couple of seconds the Edit window will reflect what is in that MIDI file.

▲ ***Fig. 91: Select a MIDI file to import.***

In the example, you can see the tempo has changed and there are several MIDI regions. On the top of the Display area you can see the markers indicating the different sections of the songs.

▲ ***Fig. 92: The MIDI file has been successfully imported.***

To hear those MIDI regions you will need to create some Instrument tracks and then drag the regions into them. The names of the MIDI tracks usually will clue you in to what kind of sound was being used. Now you are ready to go to work on this session.

In the next chapter, we'll learn more about-MIDI editing!

CHAPTER 10 MIDI—THE SKY'S THE LIMIT

As David Terry says on the DVD Tutorial about MIDI and MIDI editing, "the sky's the limit"! No truer words have ever been said. In fact I'll add to that by saying that the only limits you will find in using MIDI and MIDI editing in your projects is the limits of your own creativity. If you can think it, 9 times out 10 there is a way to make it happen in MIDI world.

As a composer, the MIDI package of a DAW is as important to me as it's audio capabilities. Sometimes it's more important. When Digidesign released Pro Tools LE 8, I heard a lot of buzz about the overhaul they had done on the MIDI side of the program. As soon as I went online to look at it I knew they had made a huge leap and investment into a new MIDI update.

I can say with all honesty that Pro Tools LE 8 is a powerful and intuitive composing tool equal to any production task.

Editing In MIDI World

Let's go back and open up the session with the drum and piano track. Once it's open click on the Smart tool. Place the cursor on the drum region and move it down, slowly, until it turns into the Grabber tool. When it changes into the Grabber tool double click on the region it will open up in the MIDI Editor.

▲ ***Fig. 93:** You can have more than one MIDI Editor Window opened at once, and each can be configured differently from the other.*

Since this book is a companion to the DVD and meant for the beginner, I would strongly recommend studying the Pro Tools Reference Guide on MIDI Editing.

First, place your cursor on the upside down triangle up in the far right hand corner and click on it. Choose Track List (Fig. 94).

On the left side of the window there is a keyboard and to the left of that is your track list just like the Edit window. When you want to edit on a MIDI region click on the black dots that are on the far left of the tracks list. Toggling these back and forth will hide or reveal your track.

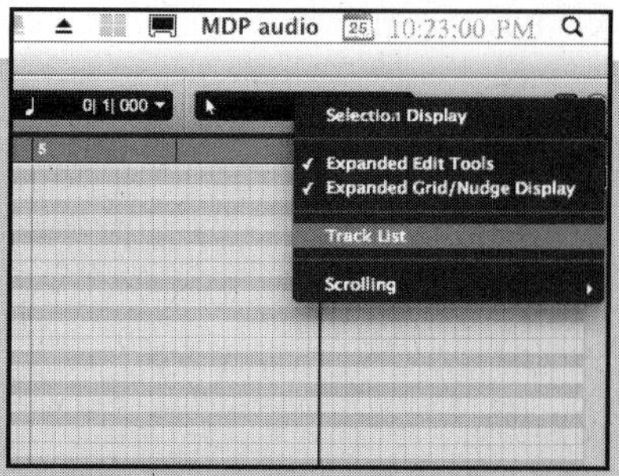

▲ ***Fig. 94: The Tracks List in the MIDI Window Editor works the same as the one in the Edit Window.***

In this example the drum track is visible.

▲ ***Fig. 95: The MIDI drum track is visible.***

If you click and hold your mouse and run it across the keys of the keyboard you will hear your drum sounds. This will help in locating not just the sound, but the actual note name.

Notes are represented by the little rectangles and squares you're seeing. To the left at the top of the keyboard there are two little boxes with colored lines running through them. These assign Color Coding to your notes. Toggling the top box turns the actual track color on and off. Toggling the box below the top one turns the Color Coding by Velocity on and off. In this example the Color Coding by Velocity is turned on. When this function is on, the notes in your track will all be a hue of red. The more vibrant and colorful, the stronger the velocity. The lighter and paler the color, the weaker the velocity.

Select the Magnifying tool and zoom in to your notes where about two measures are showing. At the bottom of the editor there is another small section running along the bottom. Place your cursor between the two sections until it turns into a bar with arrows pointing up and down. Click, hold, and pull up the bottom section. This is where much of the editing of MIDI notes is done. These are called lanes and behave just like lanes in the Edit window.

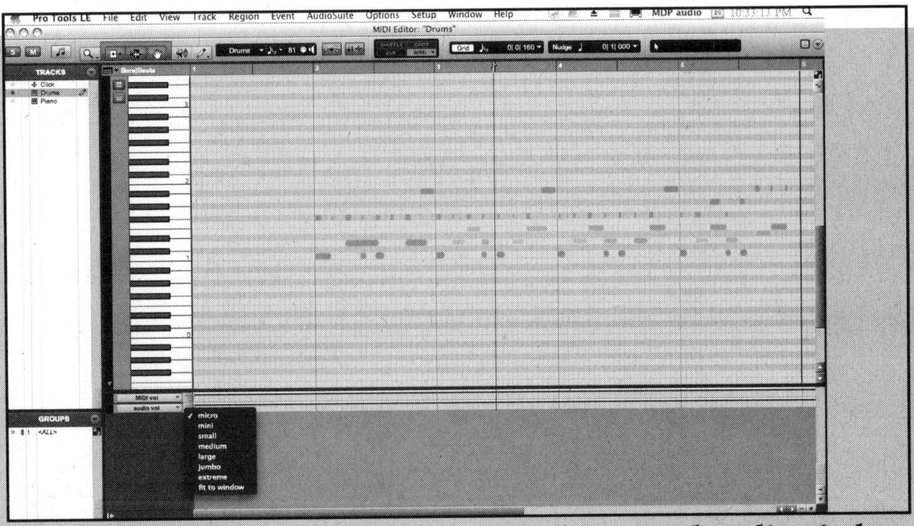

▲ ***Fig. 96: MIDI lanes behave just like lanes in the Edit window.***

Go ahead and quantize the drums first before we edit anything else.

Clicking on the lanes will bring up a menu of all the different attributes that can be edited. For brevity's sake we'll just edit velocity and volume.

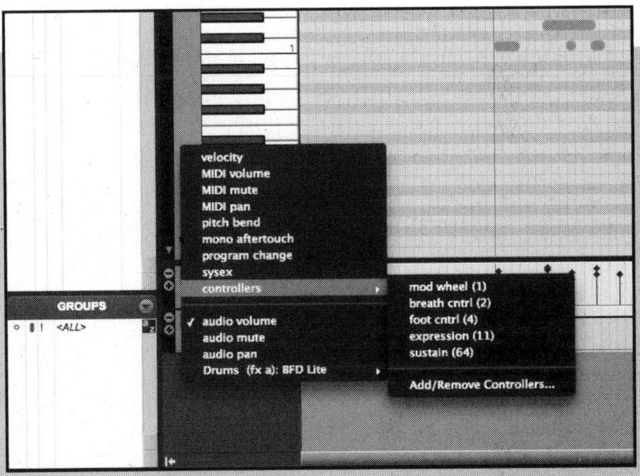

▲ ***Fig. 97: Select the attribute you wish to edit.***

Use the zoom bar to make the lanes bigger if you need to.

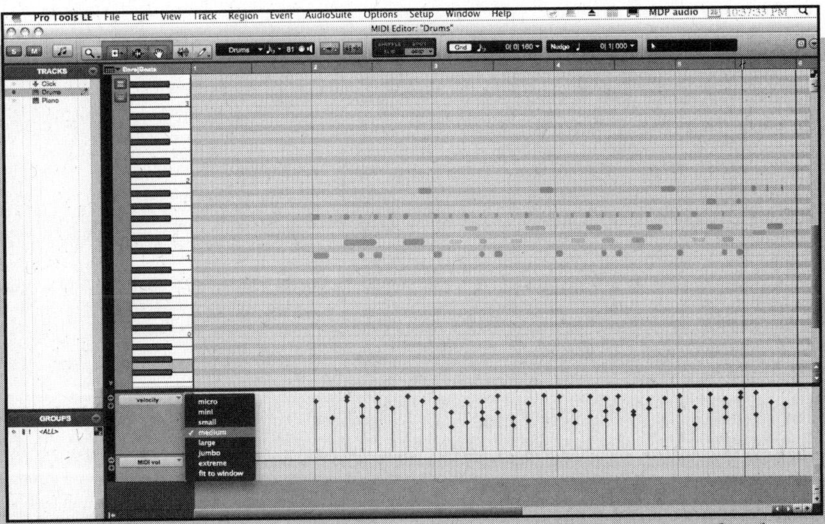

▲ ***Fig. 98: Use the Zoom bar to change the size of a lane.***

In the velocity lane, velocity is represented by the lines drawn underneath the notes. The taller the line the stronger the velocity. The notes are represented by small diamond shapes. In this example, when you see three diamond shapes on one line, that means there are three notes hitting at the same time. Each individual note velocity is represented by the placement of the diamond shape on the velocity line.

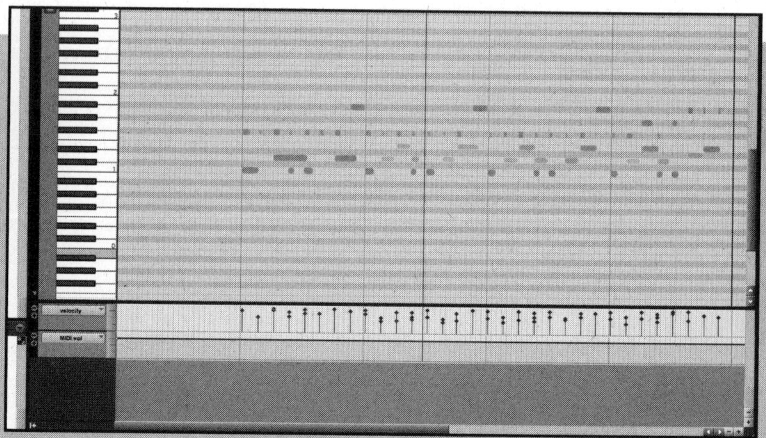

▲ ***Fig. 99: Each note hass a corresponding velocity line.***

Choose the Smart tool and place your cursor on one of the diamond shapes. The cursor will turn into a pointing finger. Click, hold, and drag up and down and you will hear that note (drum sample) going up and down in volume. You'll see a little box in the top left-hand corner of the lane with a number readout of the velocity.

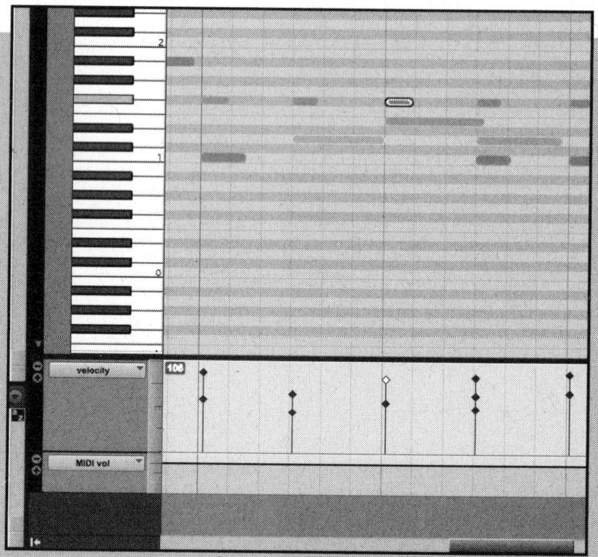

▲ ***Fig. 100: Drag the velocity line to set the velocity for each note.***

You can edit a section of notes by placing the cursor in the MIDI editor page, then clicking, holding and dragging across the notes you want to edit.

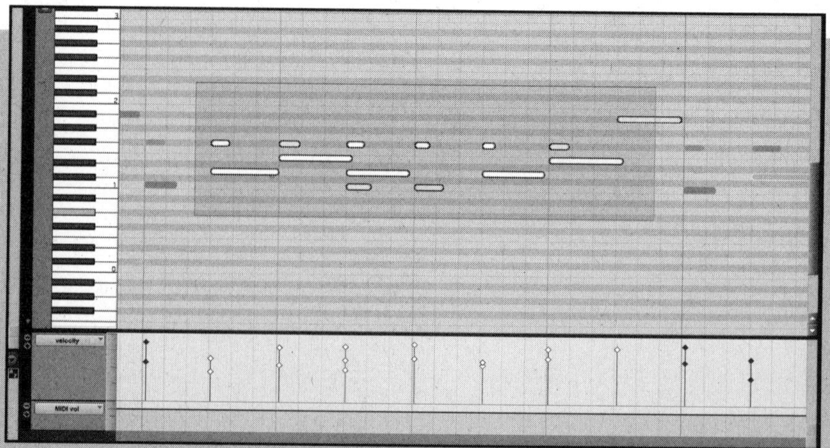

▲ ***Fig. 101: You can edit several notes at once.***

Instead of changing velocity you can automate the volume of the MIDI instrument to go up and down. Change the zoom level of the volume lane to a larger view.

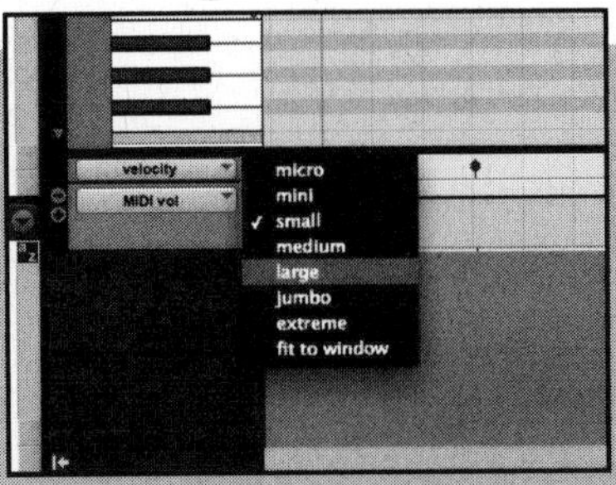

▲ ***Fig. 102: Zoom in to edit the MIDI velocity.***

Select the Pencil tool, which we haven't used yet. Click and hold on the Pencil Tool icon. A menu will reveal that there are several types of pencil cursors.

▲ ***Fig. 103: Select the Pencil tool.***

Choose Freehand and the cursor turns into a pencil. Click and draw a line across the volume lane and you will see the effect it has.

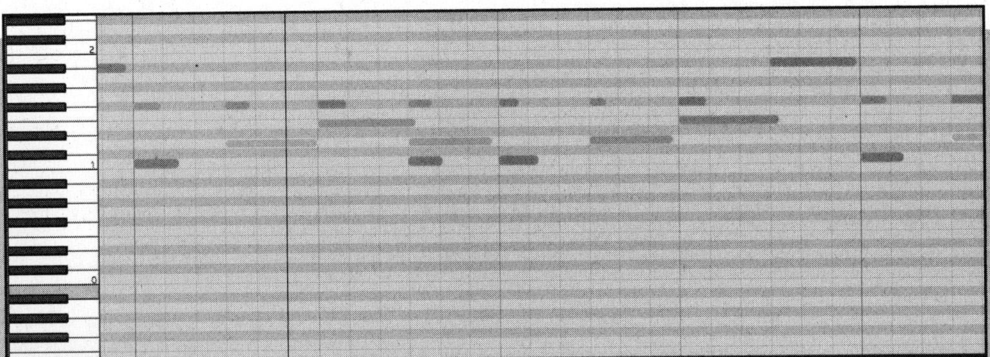

▲ ***Fig. 104: Use the Pencil tool to draw a volume curve.***

Select the measures you want to hear and press play. The other pencil cursors are for more MIDI editing. Read your Pro Tools Reference Guide for more information.

You can access all these functions through the Edit window if you want. Close the MIDI Editor window to reveal the Edit Window.

Here's another way to Zoom. Hold down the Option key when you select from the zoom bar on the track and it will make all the tracks the same size (Fig. 105).

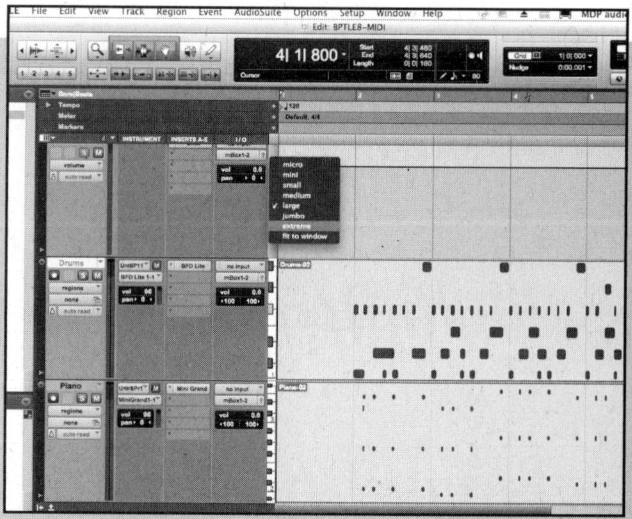

▲ *Fig. 105: Hold down the Option key while zooming to make all tracks the same size.*

Click on the Regions box on the Piano track and you will see a list of different timeline views you can choose from for that track.

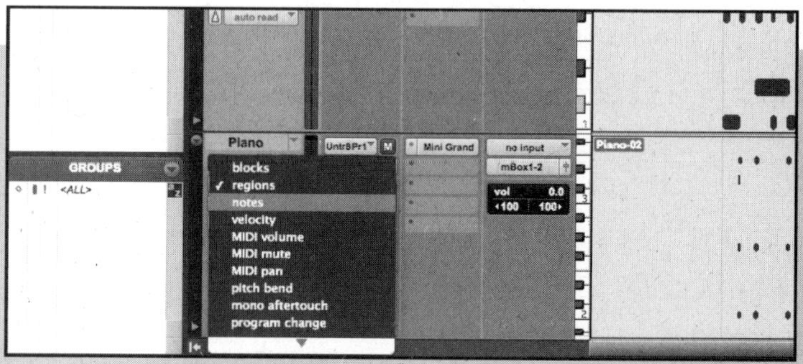

▲ *Fig. 106: Choose a Timeline view.*

Choose notes and you get a MIDI editor type view of the track. You can edit the notes right there in the track

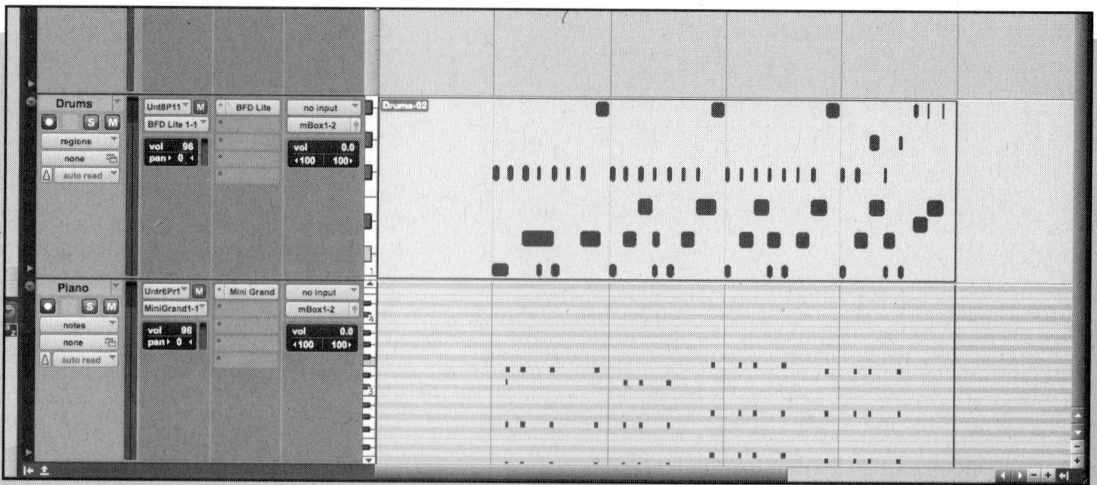

▲ *Fig. 107: Notes can be edited directly in the track.*

In figure 108, you can see the notes but the velocity view has been chosen. So now you can edit the velocity and you can right click on the region and have access to all your tools and more.

▲ ***Fig. 108: Many other tools, such as velocity, are available.***

These are great examples of how much information can be contained in MIDI files and how many different items you can edit. You can even automate certain functions of a device and then export that information in the form of MIDI files to some else. When they import your files, their MIDI devices will respond to the MIDI data that you programmed. It's really amazing!

CHAPTER 11 MIDI—IT'S ALL IN THE MIX

Mixing is an art form. There are many engineers who just mix for a living. They have their own style and sound and that's what the get hired for. Many of those engineers use Pro Tools as their main mixing system. With the DVD and this book, we're going to show you some of the basic concepts of mixing in Pro Tools LE. Who knows? Maybe one day you will be one of those engineers that everybody wants to mix their project…it can happen!

Getting Started

We have already covered several items in earlier chapters that we need to repeat here. In order to understand some of the techniques for mixing in Pro Tools, you need something to mix. After you have recorded several tracks of various instruments and vocals, get them ready for mix by consolidating any files that contain multiple regions. This is so that when you import the files to be mixed, they will all start at bar one. First create a blank session and set the bit rate and sample rate according to the files you are importing. Once the session has opened with your files, either import a MIDI file that comes with the audio files with the relevant tempo and markers information, or if you know what tempo the song was recorded in, manually set it by the Events window or by double clicking on the red tag on the main display timcline and setting it in the pop up window.

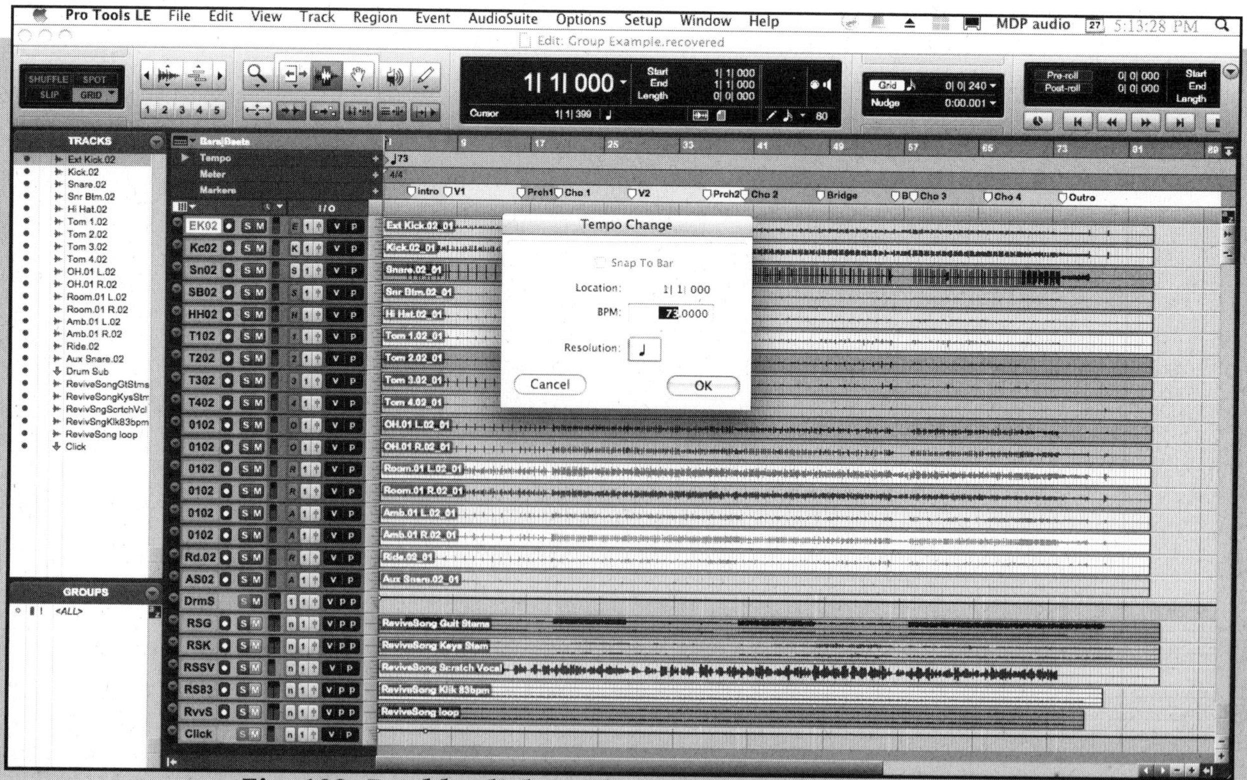

▲ *Fig. 109: Double click on the red tag in the tempo lane to set the tempo.*

Make sure you are in Grid Mode in the Edit Mode display and that the grid division line selector button is on (the grid button to the right of the counter display) so that you can see your division lines on the Edit page.

As you mix, you will be adding all kinds of effects plug-ins and time based effect plug-ins. Reverb and Delay plug-ins require a large amount of processing power. You will also be writing a huge amount of automation data. Raising the buffer size to its highest setting will help take the strain of your computer so that you can continue to work without getting those annoying error messages and ensure that your computer is working at its highest performance possible.

To set the Buffer size, click on Setup in the main menu and choose Playback Engine. From there click on the H/W Buffer Size and change it to its highest settings.

In this example an older mBox is the connected audio device. You probably have a different device so your settings may look a little different, however, the concept is still exactly the same.

Import your tracks by going to File, Audio, and then in the pop up window you will direct the software to where your files are. They will need to be converted to Pro Tool files if they haven't already. If you need a reminder, revisit Chapter 6 about Importing Audio.

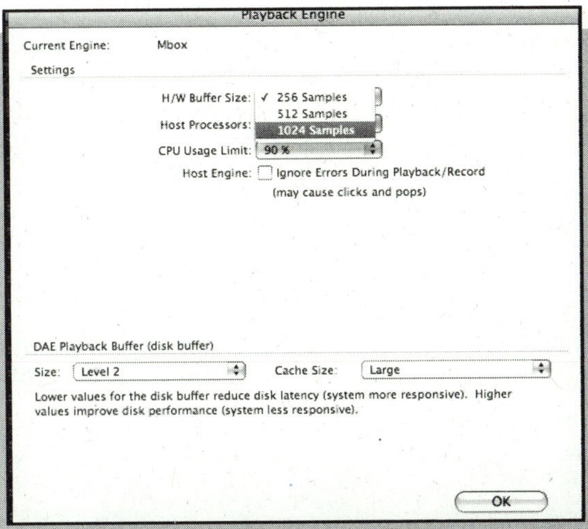

▲ *Fig. 110: Change the Buffer size to the highest setting when in Mix mode.*

After you import your tracks, a window will then open asking you if you want the files that are now in the regions list placed into their prospective tracks. Choose Track and Session Start. Here is how our example looks at the start.

▲ *Fig. 111: This Edit window is ready for mixing.*

Get Organized

Most of the time when you are importing audio files from friends or studios or other places, the tracks will not be in the order you desire on your Edit page like the previous example.

All you have to do is click and hold on the track (not the region) and pull it up or down to the position where you want it. So the first thing to do is to get your drum files in one spot. You don't have to start at this point but starting with drums is a way many mix engineers start putting their mix together. Arrange groupings of similar files, like guitars, keys, and vocals.

▲ ***Fig. 112: Rearrange the tracks to an order that makes sense.***

Color-code the tracks in a way that makes sense to you. It will make mixing much easier.

▲ ***Fig. 113: Color-coding will make your life much easier.***

The Mix Page

A few chapters back it was said that there are two main pages that you work off in Pro Tools. We've been working extensively in the Edit page. It's time now to take a look at the Mix page.

You can choose either page from the main menu under Window or the easiest method is Apple =. If you hold the Apple key down and keep pressing the equal sign, the pages will toggle back and forth. If you want to see both pages go under Window in the main menu, select Arrange and you will be given four choices of how the windows interact with each other.

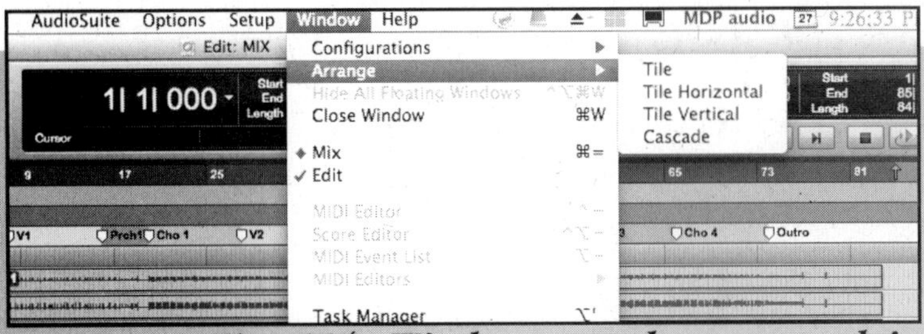

▲ *Fig. 114: Windows can be arranged in four different ways.*

Open the Mix window and take a look around. It has all of the same inputs, outputs, and other items just like the Edit page. There is a Mix Window View selector at the bottom left hand corner of the Mix window so that you can filter out some the inserts and other item that are not being used in the track.

In this example the tracks were recorded in a different studio so some of the plug-ins that were used there are not present in this mBox system. It's not a problem; you just want the audio files because you are going to use your own plug-ins on this mix.

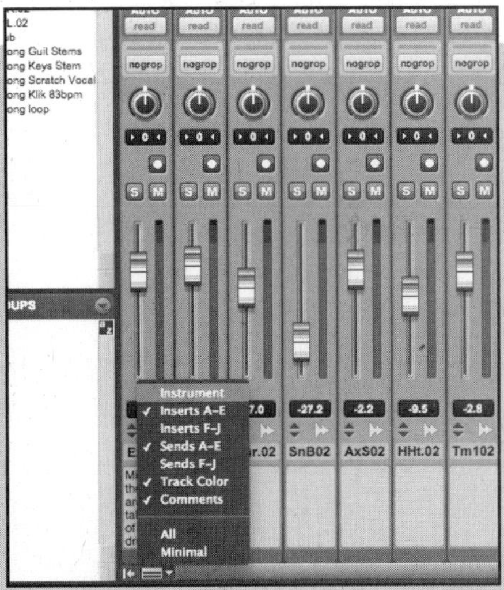

▲ *Fig. 115: Mix Window View selector.*

Go into Preferences under the File menu and make sure the Tool Tips is checked. This is very valuable in learning what all the different buttons and triangles are for. Just hold your cursor on one of those buttons and a small yellow description box will fade in.

Once the box is open if you slowly move it around you will see description boxes on almost every item. This works on all the pages in Pro Tools.

▲ *Fig. 116: Use the Tool Tips to learn your way around all the functions of Pro Tools.*

There are two very important functions that you will use in the Mix page. The Sends and Auxiliary inputs. Let's talk about Auxiliary inputs first. They can be used for effects returns, creating a sub mix, or as a bus master.

Groups

In the example we want to take all the cymbals and sub group them into its own stereo mix. What's so great about this? Instead of dealing with seven different track faders, we can now control them with one stereo fader. The first thing to do is create and Auxiliary track. Go to the same menu where you create audio and instrument tracks (Track-New) and choose from the menu list Aux Input. The track will be inserted into your mixer. Since we are going to control the cymbals with this Aux Input, we will select, hold and drag the Aux strip over next to the tracks that we are going to group. Be sure and name it. In this example it's labeled as Cym Master.

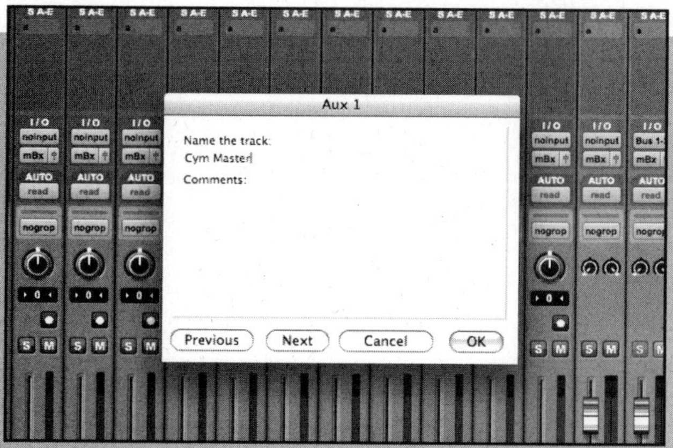

▲ ***Fig. 117: Using an Auxiliary Input as a Group Master.***

Hold down Shift and select the tracks you want to group. Click the Group List pop-up button in the Groups List box and select New Groups and you will get the Create Groups window.

From this window you can edit the groups to control items such as Mutes and Solos. By checking Edit and Mix, Edit, or Mix, groups can be linked to the Edit and Window pages or have separate attributes depending on which page you are in. You can name your groups here and give them an identity letter. The tracks on the right represent the present group you are putting together. If you are missing a track, select it from the left side and click Add. You can also remove tracks from your group on this page.

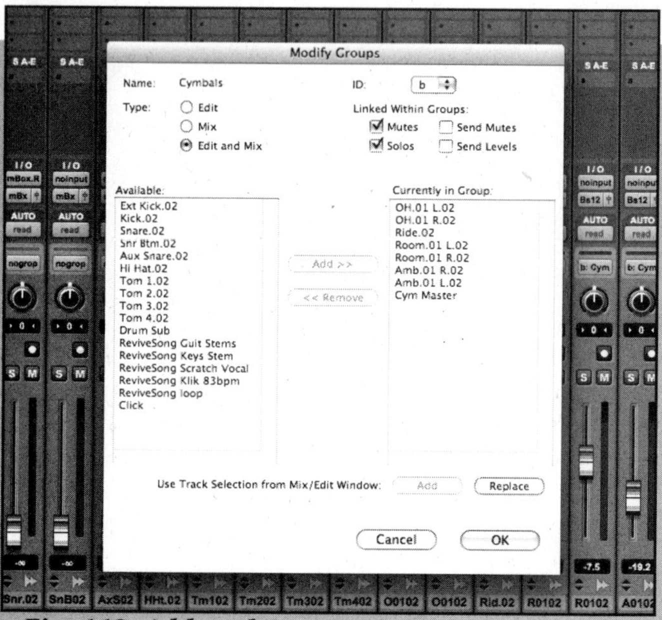

▲***Fig. 118: Add and remove groups to your group.***

When you are finished click OK and the Cymbals group will be in the Groups List box.

▲ ***Fig. 119: All Groups you create will be located here.***

If you want to color-code your group, double click at the top of the strip and the color palette will open. Choose groups from the menu and choose color. You can see the name of the group and the color of the group just above the pan control.

Now the grouped faders must have their outputs assigned to the input of the Aux Input or in this example the Cymbals Master. The tracks should still be highlighted. While holding down the Shift and Option keys select one of the outputs of the grouped tracks. Select from the menu Interface and then you will see a list of bus assignments. Choose Bus1-2 (stereo).

▲ Fig. 120: All the outputs in your system should be present here. If not recheck the I/O options under the Setups main menu.

Now all the outputs should say Bs12. The outputs are now being directed to the inputs of Bus 1, which is a stereo input. Go to the Aux Input you have created and assign the input to Bus 1-2. In this example we will assign the inputs of the Cymbal Master to Bus 1-2 thereby directing the outputs of all the cymbals through this stereo track.

▲ Fig. 121: The same thing should be true for the inputs. They should all appear here assuming your I/O is setup correctly.

Leave the Aux Input Master volume level at 0.0 (or less if you want). Play your track and adjust the levels of your grouped tracks to where you think it sounds right. Click on the Group Lists pop up button and select Modify Groups. Select from the Identity menu your group, add your Aux Input master to the list and click OK.

When you move the Aux Input master or in this example the Cymbals Master, all the faders of the group will follow the master. You can also insert effects in the Aux Input track that will affect all the faders that are grouped to it, or you can go to just one of the tracks in the group and insert effects on that track only. You can also have a subgroup of faders in a larger set of grouped faders. To learn more about all the different applications for using groups, consult the Pro Tools Preference Guide.

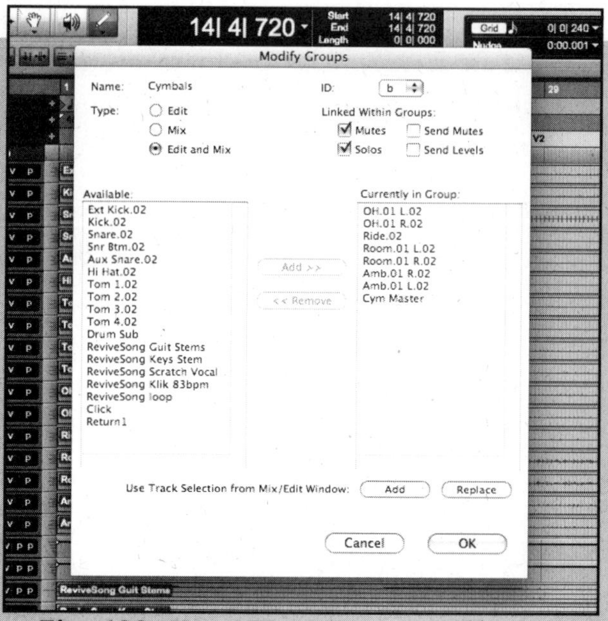

▲ ***Fig. 122: Your Master now will control all the faders in the Group.***

Sends

A send is basically what it says it is—it "sends" the audio of the track to a specified point. That could be a group, sub mix, or an effects return.

In this example a send will be used to send the audio from a snare track to an effects return that has a reverb insert. First, create another stereo Auxiliary Input. Remember that Aux Inputs in Pro Tools are used for many things including effects returns.

Locate the new Aux input on your mixer. Double click on the name Aux 1 and name it Return 1 or Reverb 1 or whatever you want. Click on the input for the Return 1 track and choose bus and then choose Bus 3-4(Stereo) since we are already using Bus 1-2 for our cymbal group.

▲ ***Fig. 123: You can use Auxiliary Inputs for all kinds of effects Returns.***

Scroll to the top of the mixer window where you see "I A-E". These are the first five slots for inserting plug-ins. Click on the first slot, choose multi-channel plug-in, Reverb, and then select whatever Reverb you want to choose.

▲ *Fig. 124: Select a reverb to insert.*

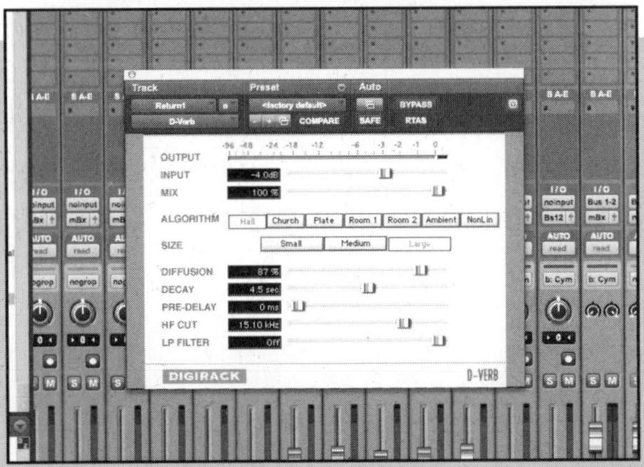

▲ *Fig. 125: There are many different types of plug-ins with a multitude of options. Don't be afraid to experiment!*

In this example we are going to send our snare track to bus 3-4, the reverb return. On the snare track, go to "S A-E" which is just below the inserts, choose bus, then bus 3 (mono) because this is a mono track.

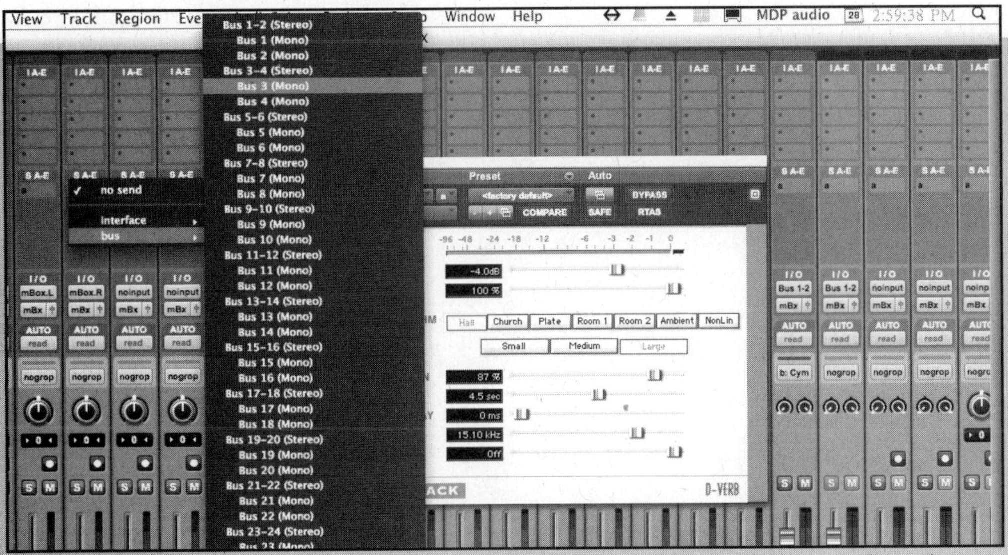

▲ *Fig. 126: Send the snare track to bus 3.*

A miniature fader will come up which is the send fader.

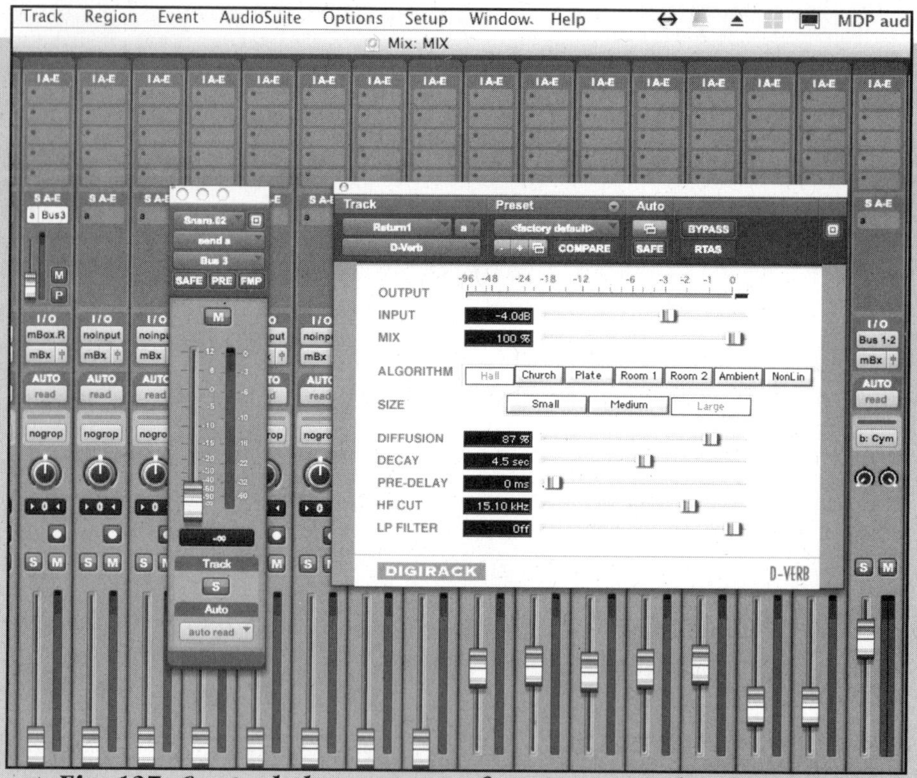

▲ *Fig. 127: Control the amount of snare to send using the fader.*

There is a button labeled P on the send fader. This is the Pre and Post toggle switch. Post fader sends to the reverb based on the value of the snare fader. If the snare fader is all the way down there is no send level. If you select Pre fader, the send fader becomes independent of the snare fader so even if the snare fader is off, the send fader still sends to the reverb return. This is used when you want to hear just the reverb return without the original source mixed in with it.

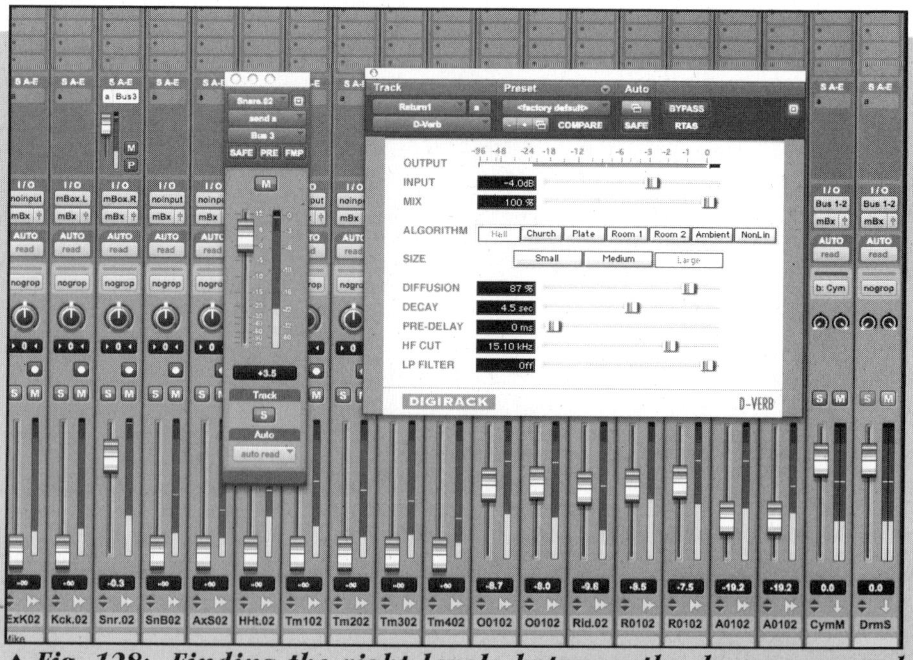

▲ *Fig. 128: Finding the right levels between the dry source and the wet source is critical to a good mix.*

Automation!

This is the really incredible part of the digital audio revolution. Just a few years ago analog consoles were fitted with VCA or Flying Fader automation packages. VCA (Voltage Control Amplifier) was basically done with recorded digital signals from a moving fader or on and off switch. Flying Faders were actual mechanically controlled faders. With these two systems and others, you could control fader levels, mutes, and any switch that could be turned on and off. Some newer consoles had the ability to take digital snapshots and change many of the send levels and other level controllers. But Pro Tools and other Digital Audio Workstations have revolutionized the meaning and capability of automated mixing.

We are going to cover just the very basics of mixing in Pro Tools LE. The thing to remember is that everything, and I mean everything can be automated.

You can record the automation by putting the automation in Write mode, move a fader, then put it in Read mode and it will remember what you did and play it back exactly how you did it. Another method is to use the pencil tool and actually write your automation into the track manually. Let's look at both methods.

Write and Read Method

Be sure and watch the DVD so that you will be able to see the faders moving. It's a little bit difficult to show that in a book!

Go to the Edit page, select any track that you want to work on and click on the Track View selector where it says waveform, and select volume.

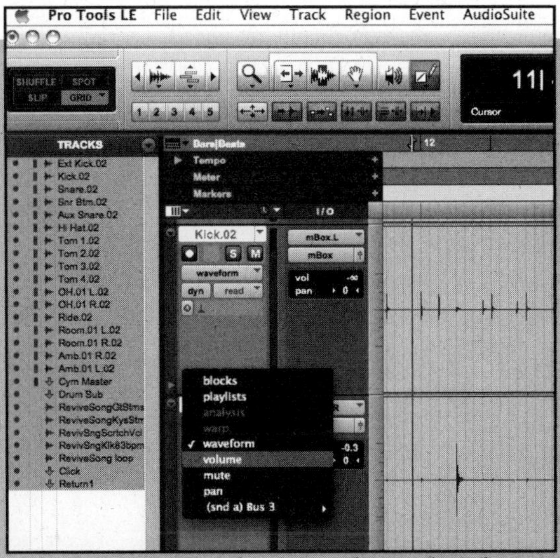

▲ ***Fig. 129: The Timeline display is a great way to get a visual on many items that you are editing.***

Then click on the Automation Mode selector where it says Read and select Write.

▲ *Fig. 130: Select Write mode.*

Write will be in red and you should see a dark line running through the track now.

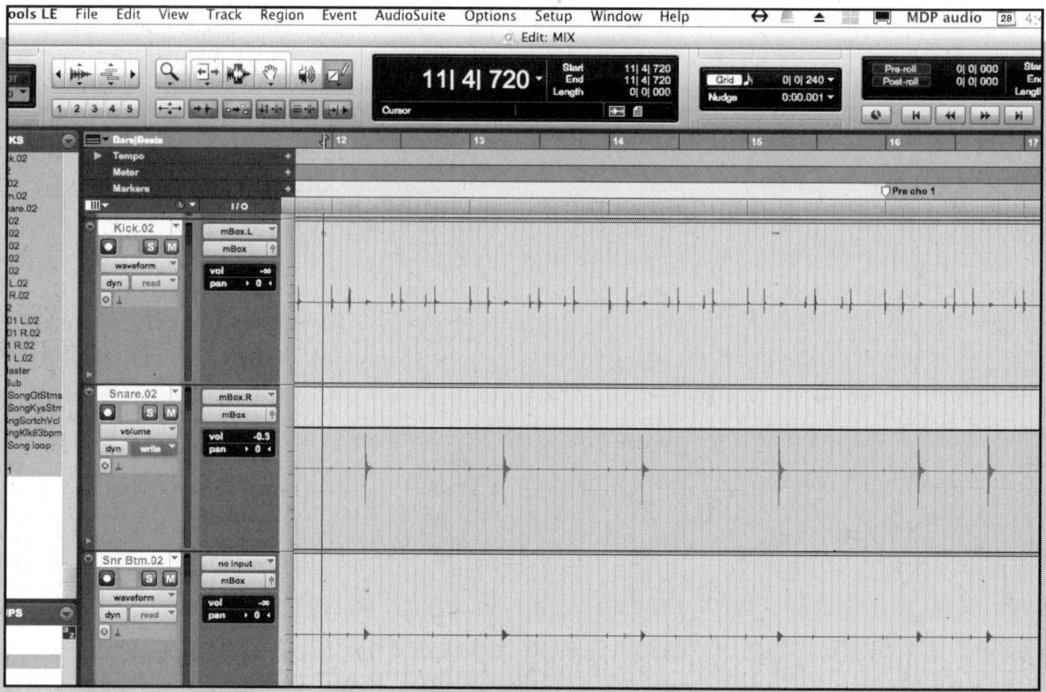

▲ *Fig. 131: The snare track is in Write mode.*

Press play and move the fader up and down and you will see a red line appear in your track that is following your movements.

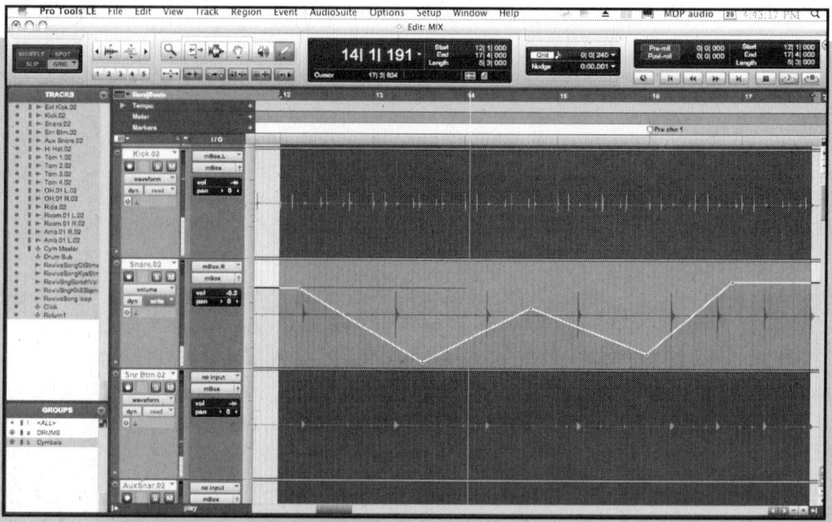

▲ *Fig. 132: The red line follows the movements of the fader.*

Hit stop and you will see what you have recorded.

The Automation selector will say Latch. For now click on it and select Read. Select the section to loop, press play and then Apple = to look at your mix page, and what you'll see is the fader moving up and down.

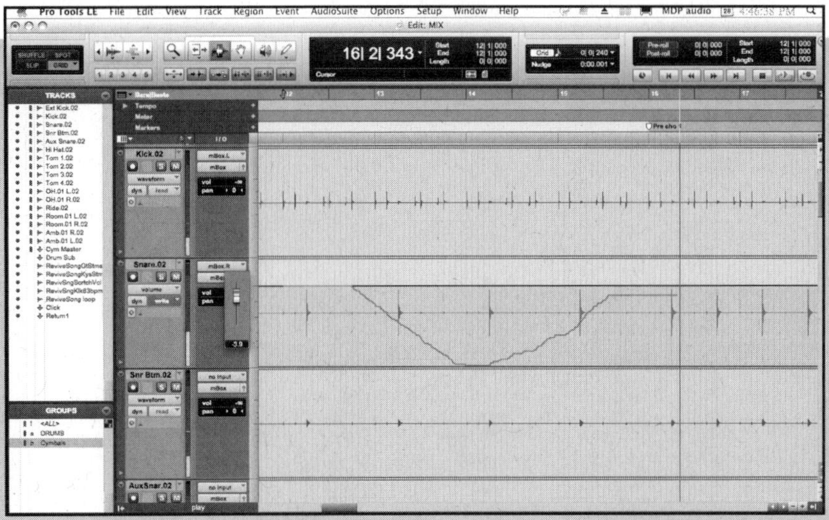

▲ ***Fig. 133: Automation was successfully recorded.***

Freehand Method

To write automation manually, just select the pencil tool from the tool bar or by right clicking and selecting from the menu. There are several styles of pencil to choose from but for now select Freehand.

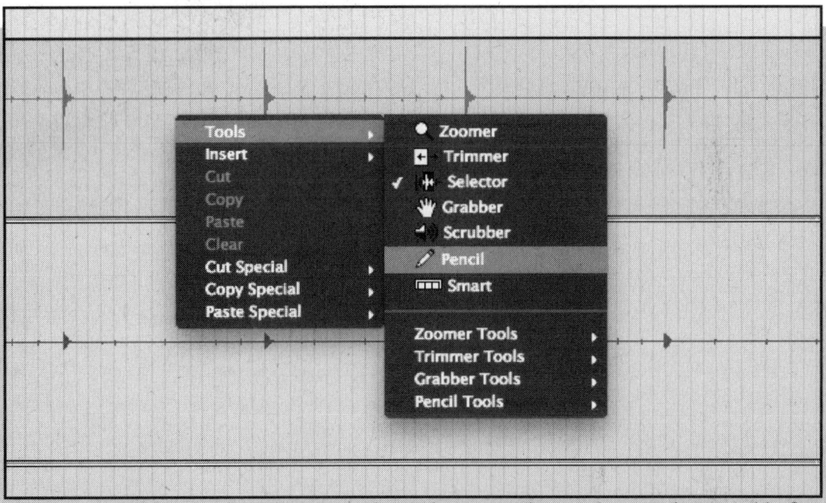

▲ ***Fig. 134: The Freehand Pencil tool works well for capturing natural moves.***

Take the pencil and click, hold and then drag the place that you want to change. When you do a new automation line will appear.

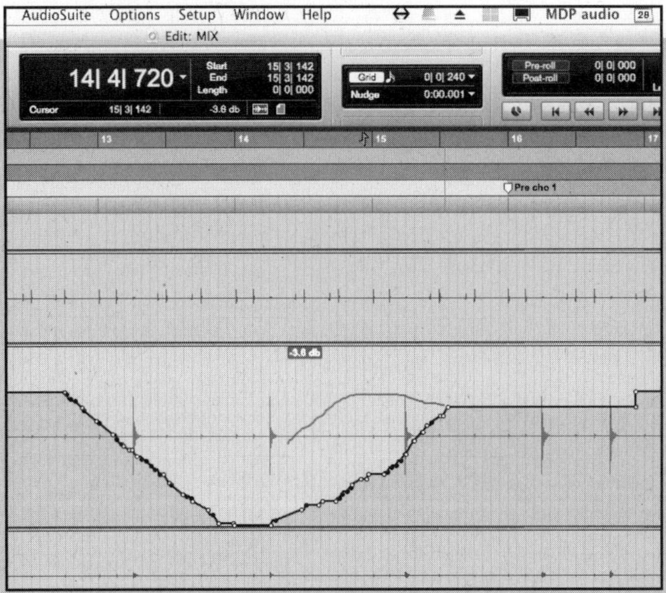

▲ ***Fig. 135: Use the Pencil to draw a new automation line.***

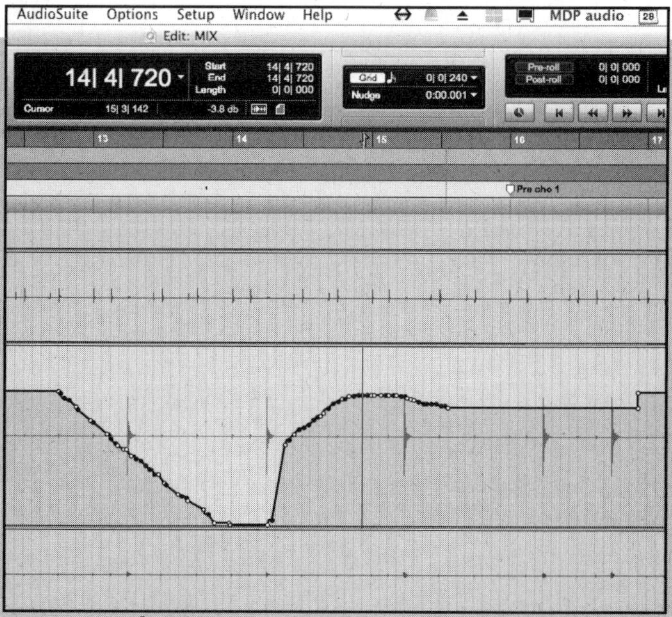

▲ *Fig. 136: The result of automation using the Pencil tool.*

You can do this to effects, masters, subs, groups and on and on. And by using the Pencil tool you can refine a mix to perfection.

Share It

Pretty soon you will need to let everyone start hearing your projects so here's how you do it.

Bounce to Disk takes everything you have recorded, edited and mixed and burns it into a stereo track for you to burn a CD or make an mp3. You don't have to set up tracks. Just take your cursor and select an area in the Timeline that you want to bounce. Usually that will be from measure one until the end of the song. It's best to go a little bit further than the end of the last region in case there is delay or reverb hanging over.

▲ *Fig. 137: Be sure and to start at measure one and to go past the last region.*

Once you have made your selection, Click on File, then choose Bounce To, and choose Disk.

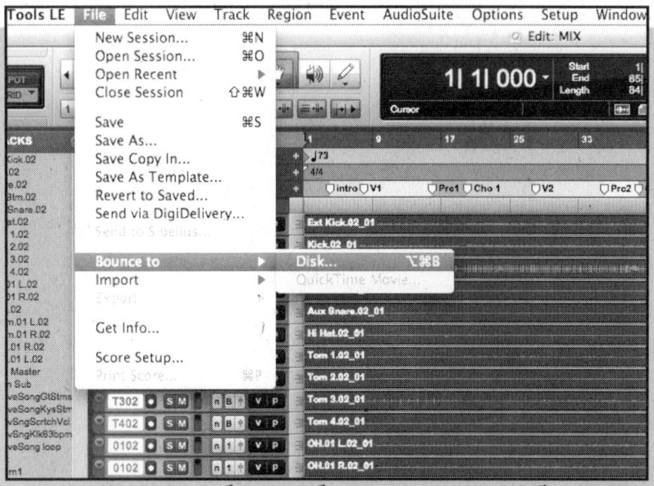

▲ *Fig. 138: Choose the Bounce to Disk option.*

You will have several options to choose from and what you choose is totally dependent on what your final needs are. In this example, MP3 was chosen.

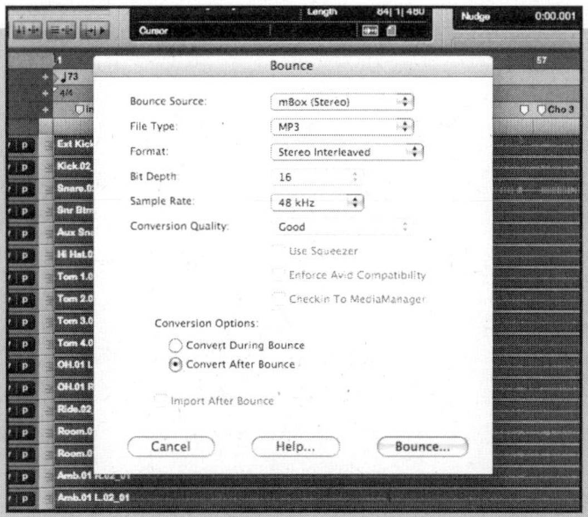

▲ *Fig. 139: There are many options to choose from. Be sure and have the right ones selected!*

Pro Tools LE automatically loads some of the parameters in for certain settings but you can change those to what ever you need. When you have finished making your selections click Bounce. You will need to direct where the Bounce will be stored. The Bounce is done in realtime which means it will play it from top to bottom. Once it is done go find it and burn a CD or upload it to the web and let everyone hear your creation. Be sure and keep the Pro Tools LE Reference Guide handy. It's full of great information. Good Luck!

CONCLUSION

Pro Tools LE is a power packed digital audio recorder combined with a newly upgraded MIDI sequencing package. The features include the ability to record, arrange, compose, edit, mix, and master professional quality projects for all types of music, video, film and multimedia applications. This book along with the DVD will give you the basic tools to get you on your way to fulfilling your musical dreams.

ABOUT THE AUTHOR

Michael Demus moved to Nashville in 1984 and has been in the studio/production business since 1989 under the name Michael D. Productions. The Music Box is his home studio that he works out of most of the time. Michael and his wife Nancy have traveled the world with several different music outreach ministries and hope to spend the next few years in South Africa. They have been married for 32 years.

To see the Music Box and to find out more about Michael you can visit his webpage michaeldemus.com or listen to his newest project on FaceBook at MDP Projects.

INDEX